HEALING WITH HORSES

Growth and Transformation through the Way of the Horse

To Mary & Paul

Life is sunny with
a chance of tornado
TN!

Jennifer

HEALING WITH HORSES

Growth and Transformation through the Way of the Horse

A Collection of Inspirational Stories from the FEEL Alumni
Association: Beverley Clifton, Susan Collard, Wilma de Zeeuw,
Jennifer Garland, Wendy Golding, Jackie Ladouceur,
Andre Leclipteux, Jennifer Schramm,
Raymonde Violette, and Kera Willis

Big Country Publishing, LLC

Healing with Horses, Growth and Transformation through the Way of the Horse
Copyright© 2015 by FEEL Alumni
Library of Congress Control Number: 2015900932
ISBN: 978-1-938487-13-2

Front Cover Photo of Thor: Andre Leclipteux
Back Cover Photo of Rosa: Andre Leclipteux
Warriors of the Heart© Jackie Ladouceur, Know Thyself, Be True© Jennifer Schramm Living my Soul's Calling© Wendy Golding, What Brings Me Joy© Susan Collard, You Just Don't Make That Stuff Up© Wilma de Zeeuw, The Invitation© Andre Leclipteux, Emotions, Messages, and Healing Horses© Beverley Clifton, Power of Emotions© Raymonde Violette, Sunny with a Chance of Tornado© Jennifer Garland, How Much We Can Love© Kera Willis, Where the Magic Begins© Wendy Golding.

Published by
Big Country Publishing, LLC
7691 Shaffer Parkway, Suite C
Littleton, CO 80127
USA
www.bigcountrypublishing.com
Printed in the United States of America, U.K. and Australia

*For all of the horses who grace us
with their wisdom and transform our world.*

TABLE OF CONTENTS

ACKNOWLEDGMENTS

The stories in this book are true accounts of powerful healing experienced with horses. Some of the people's names have been changed to pseudonyms.

In gratitude we thank the FEEL Alumni Steering committee without whose inspiration this book would never have come to pass. At the time of this book's inception, the Steering committee was comprised of Deborah Bonk, Wendy Golding, Alla Hirsch, Heather Kerr, Jackie Ladouceur, Andre Leclipteux, and Wilma de Zeeuw.

With immense appreciation we acknowledge the unstinting support and vision of our publisher and editor Christina Winslow. She has brought our writing to life and has truly connected to the spirit of the horse. We all thank Christina for her invaluable wisdom and passion as she mentored each of us on our writing journey.

FORWARD

"If you reach deeply into your own heart and the heart of others, understanding will arise. If there is understanding, acceptance and love will follow, and suffering will be eased."
—Thich Nhat Hanh

Many, many years ago our ancestors sat around the fire sharing stories to inspire and support each other. Gathered with them were their animal companions. You might see a tabby cat sitting on the lap of an old woman, a dog by his master's feet, and grazing around the circle you would see and feel the horses that had carried them on their journey. Once in a while a horse would look up and gently come over and nudge their nose into the circle. They were and are today in relationship with us and listening with their hearts. Today, we may not literally have horses carrying us on their backs, but because of our deep relationship and kinship with them, they are willing to accompany and support us on our journeys. I believe it is because we all carry the genetic memory of shared support and stories that we rely on the horses to bring us back to our souls, our spirit, and to see with our hearts.

The FEEL (Facilitated Equine Experiential Learning)® program is an excellent testament to the power and grace that is possible when we engage and learn through the way of the horse. My years of friendship and collaboration with Wendy and Andre, their herd, and their colleagues have reinforced my belief that horses can help us rediscover what I call "the blueprint of our souls." From an authentic place of being, we can find new possibilities, and the work with the horses can help us take that first vulnerable step towards our expanded futures.

Our work in the growing field of FEEL (Facilitated Equine Experiential Learning) is often subtle and appears to the outside observer that "nothing is happening." What is happening is that the facilitator and the horse engage with the client in mutual exploration and practice the concept I have named "Holding the Sacred Space of Possibility." The sacred space is that place between, the sacred pause where grace and guidance happens. Together, the facilitator and the horse create a container of support that is a fully engaged form of patience that is crucial to finding innovative solutions to activate the authentic self. This is the place where healing emerges and the person and the horse can reclaim and embrace their souls' blueprint.

I have often witnessed a client coming out of a quiet session with the horse and heard them say: "It was magic! I felt like myself for the first time. My heart just opened and these tears came flowing out—but they felt free, open —you know not jammed up in my throat". You will be reading about many other stories like this as you travel the pages of this book. It may look like magic; however, it is a process scientists can now actually name which happens only in relationship. What the client and others felt, saw, and experienced is the limbic connection of two beings. Relationship does affect the revision of these pathways in the brain through the processes of limbic resonance, limbic regulation, and limbic revision or restructuring.

The General Theory of Love, a book by Lewis, Amini, and Lannon shows us how the limbic connection and being in relationship can offer healing and change.

The first part of emotional healing is being limbically known [limbic resonance]...having someone with a keen ear catch your melodic essence...a precise seer's light can still split the night, illuminate treasures long lost, and dissolve many fearsome figures into shadows and dust. Limbic regulation happens through relationship. But people do not learn emotional modulation as they do geometry or the names of state capitals. These concepts are stored in the neocortical brain. People and animals absorb the skill from living in the presence of an adept external modulator, and they learn it implicitly.

I can't begin to tell you how passionate I have become about some of the newest brain and body research and information coming from very reliable and dedicated scientists and clinicians. Most of my professional life, I have practiced as a clinician whether I am conducting a session as a psychotherapist, coach, mentor, or teacher. The many "miracles" I have been a part of, fill me with awe and hope for the ability of people to learn new things, change, and have better lives.The work that I do with the horses has transferred to everything I do and teach since these brilliant beings are so good at helping people come back to their true selves.

Neuroplasticity of the brain is the term used to describe the capacity of our brain for creation of new neural connections and for growing new neurons in response to experience. In the process of experiential learning with the horses, the experience itself—which is very new for most people, i.e. being with a horse without doing anything— can actually assist the client in forming and developing new neural connections. I often give a simple explanation like this: The horses help the humans to see, feel, and believe in the possibility that the old super highway way of being and responding to a familiar person, stimulus, thought, or action can be replaced by a new path— much like the road less traveled. Implicit learning or knowing happens in an actual experience and thus supports our work with the horses.

The following story is an example about how the limbic connection with the horse offered possibilities which altered and changed the neural pathways of the participant. This man had a long history with the horse he was working with and was participating in an equine exercise I call Relationship in Motion (RIM). Initially he was asked to perform a goal directing the horse around a round pen. He followed the goal by visualizing where he wanted to horse to go and completed his task perfectly. He did not take into account the value of his relationship with the horse and like many of us got into the task at hand but lost his heart connection. We asked the man to go back into the round pen with the horse and find the balance between his heart, his head, and his power center. The result was amazing, you could see and feel his joy and watch the horse fully engage with ease and grace. He shared how easy this was compared to the first experience where he achieved the goal but lost the connection with his friend, the horse.

This man was a veteran who previously was housebound, out of work, and afraid because of severe Post Traumatic Stress Disorder (PTSD). He had developed PTSD after he left the service where his job was to find and dispose of hidden bombs. He was a good soldier and did what he had to do at the time for his job, his country, and for his own safety. I first met him at a workshop he attended more than two years ago, and he has worked with a program designed for returning veterans which involves the horses. The horse he worked with that day has been a huge part of his healing. It took two years of hard work with his therapist, his group, and the horses for him to be able to come to this place. After his experience I asked him if he could put into a few words what it was like for him. His simple reply still brings tears to my eyes.

"I found my soldier's heart!"

He got the implicit knowing through this exercise that he could lead with heart and fully engage, not only with the horse, but he was also able to translate his experience into his other life at work and with his family.

Seeing with the heart allows us to be in present moment awareness and to live from our authentic self. Your heart is an instrument made of extremely subtle energy. When you "feel" music, see the beauty of a flower, and hear a bird's song, you feel it through the filter of the heart. The heart controls the energy flow of opening and closing to others. The heart closes when stored energy, feelings, or unfinished business block the opening of the heart. Our work with the horses allows people to take that first step of vulnerability to open our hearts and walk the world with confidence and grace. The essence of spirituality is an inner commitment to go beyond yourself every minute of the day for the rest of your life. It is being in the vulnerable, unknowing part of you. We can decide to take the journey by letting go of these outdated beliefs, being a witness to our own thoughts, our feelings, and our state of mind. Living authentically from this soulful place is the way to true freedom.

The FEEL program led by Wendy and Andre is such an example of seeing with the heart. The herd at Horse Spirit Connections is always an integral part of each session and program. Both Wendy and Andre will regularly consult the horses to see what ideas they may have before they move forward with any new idea or project. I have known them both since 2004 and have worked with the FEEL training program since its inception in 2008. The quality of the program and the facilitators that graduate are exemplary examples of what is best in the field of Equine Facilitated Learning and Therapy.

Kathleen Barry Ingram, MA BCC

www.sacredplaceofpossibility.com

INTRODUCTION
Magical Connections with Horses

Sometimes we experience incredible and astonishing moments that go far beyond what our mind and senses can accept. These astonishing occasions are genuine experiences of the unexplainable. Being in the presence of a horse inspires a sense of mystery and wonder, allowing magic to occur. If you love horses, dream of horses, or are simply drawn to horses this book is for you.

The FEEL (Facilitated Equine Experiential Learning)® Alumni Association is proud to present these inspirational horse stories highlighting the extraordinary connection between two species—horses and humans.

You are invited to take this exciting journey with the horses. Our stories are not about riding these majestic beings, they are about connecting with horses in an entirely different way. We meet and interact with them from the ground without saddles, bridles, halters, or lead ropes. We honor the horses for their incredibly sage wisdom and meet them on an equal footing, one being to another.

What does this connection look like? How can we relate to an animal that is so much bigger and stronger than we are? Standing close to a horse can make you feel exceedingly small and insignificant next to their powerful presence with their enormous body, four long legs, long neck, and massive head soaring high above. Our human naturalness is to flee or try and control something that inspires fear.

Instead we invite you to let the horse BE the epitome of freedom and power that has captured man's imagination throughout thousands of years. As you will read, the horse is so willing and wanting to connect with humans; however, they urge us to be present with them in the way which was second nature to us in our childhood: fully open without judgment or expectations, trusting our heart's innate knowing, following our instincts. Meeting them at liberty, the horse is free to move and respond based on how they perceive us, whether it is coming closer to us or moving farther away. The horses reflect back to us the "real" person we are inside. The horses nurture this deepening relationship with our authentic self as this is the person they desire to connect with.

Being with a horse inspires a heart connection. This opening of our hearts creates the space for incredible healing, connecting with our power, and living with joy. They empower us to create a life of beauty, freedom, and power from a heart-centered way of being.

As you read these narratives, hear the whispers of the horses talking to you. Let the horses re-awaken your body's innate wisdom and healing ability as they connect with you on a mental, physical, emotional, and spiritual level. Let your heart open to new possibilities.

The incredible transformative power of this intimate connection with horses is hard to understand without experiencing it firsthand. The following are quotes from participants whose lives were changed from their experiences with the horse teachers.

"When I came I wasn't really sure what to expect. I figured that I would be learning some interesting things about what horses can teach in general. I was absolutely amazed at what they revealed to me about myself. I usually try to hide my thoughts and keep them to myself. As soon as I arrived here it seemed like the wall was taken down and I wasn't allowed to rebuild it. I had to look at my true self and my true thoughts and really understand them. It was a safe place to do that."

— Dawn Addison, Alliston, Ontario

"Through my interactions with the horses, the realizations and transformations have been life changing. My heart is opening to give and to receive with so much light and love... and acceptance. They have held a safe space for me to learn

about myself and love myself. Some of us can search for that forever, and I can't articulate how appreciative and thankful I am."

—Gini Buckman, Acton, Ontario

"An introduction to the magical-ness of nature that I cannot recommend highly enough. I experienced firsthand the intelligence and wisdom of horses, the way they artfully mirror your emotions and communicate the information you need to know. The result is an opening to a whole other dimension of experience for that I am grateful. Wonderful!"

—Jeff Warren, Toronto, Ontario

"There was a remarkable transformation that happened within me this weekend and it led me to have one of the best days of my life on Monday with my children and horses. I approached and interacted with them from a place of Heart and no words exist to describe the interactions and reactions I received in return."

"After breathing beside my horses and making a connection of Spirit, one of my horses raised an eyebrow and asked, "who is this new you?" If horses could have an expression of being impressed then he sure was wearing one that night! It's pretty special stuff and no, you can't make that shit up! LOL."

—Alana, Etobicoke, Ontario

"An experience to find yourself...by listening, watching, feeling the horses. A time where your mind's energy refocuses and lets your heart see first."

—Brittany Oremush, Gatenau, QC

The authors of the following chapters are passionate about the magic the horses have brought into their lives. These profound stories highlight how the horses can similarly light up your world. Invite the horses to help you shine from the inside out!

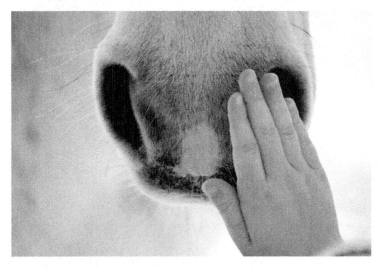

CHAPTER 1

Warriors of the Heart

By Jackie Ladouceur

There is a place that feels like home, a familiarity in the air, the stillness of the trees, and the solitude of nature and horses that infuses me with a calm and grounding sense of inner peace. The air is cool and the rays of the early morning sun are beginning to capture the beautiful and golden highlights in the changing colors of the poplar leaves. The changing colors and the heavy overnight dew are now indicative of yet another one of nature's most vibrant and plentiful seasons to pass. As the leaves begin to warm, they silently detach and float effortlessly to the ground, and I am reminded of how the natural process of change is essential for the rejuvenation of all living things.

As this early workshop morning progresses my senses are becoming more alive with the awakening of nature. A variety of chickadees and multicolored finches begin to sing an array of musical notes that naturally attunes me to the beauty and peacefulness of the world around me. There is a penetrating stillness that lies beneath the sounds and smells of nature that radiates through me, and I am encouraged to breathe more fully as I fill my lungs with the fresh, crisp fall air. As I gaze out into the field I am amazed at this time of year that there are still so many patches of brilliant yellow and purple wildflowers standing vibrantly amongst the fading wild grasses which are home to hundreds of tiny orange butterfly-like moths who have taken up residence all summer long.

As I follow the movement of the flowers lightly shifting and swaying with the directional changes of the wind, I catch my first glimpse of the day of the horses in the far corner of the pasture. After all these years of seeing horses day in and day out, I am always amazed that my heart still flutters with excitement every time I see them.

In perfect synchronization the horses react and abruptly raise their heads up from the grass. They stare for a moment to fully acknowledge my presence as they continue to chew, promptly return to grazing. Their peaceful reaction is indicative of them sensing my arrival long before I even think I was seen.

I take up residence on the ground against one of the old wooden fence posts and admire the brilliant sheen, perfectly raised dapples, and the thickening of their early autumn coats. Their manes and tails flow so gracefully in the wind and are one their most elegant and majestic symbols of their spiritual freedom and physical beauty. As I begin to look at the time they graciously remind me that time as we know does not exist for them, but what does is simply the present moment and all that moves within it. Their gifted and innate ability to easily draw us into the flow of the natural world offers us such a unique opportunity to step out of our busy realities and into the presence of our awareness so that we too can listen to the innate intelligence and wisdom that our own bodies are gifted with.

A large raven is perched at the top of an old dead tree at the far end of the field and sits silently in the stillness of the morning's rising sun. I am always delighted at the spontaneous arrival of these mysterious birds on our teaching days and am greatly inspired by their willingness to join us and the magical teachings of the herd. The medicine and wisdom of the raven knows the mysteries of life, awakens the energy of magic, and is strongly linked to the cycles of death and rebirth, which has such a powerful symbolic message at this vastly changing time of year. The arrival of assorted wildlife indigenous to the land is always a rare opportunity to explore deeper into the realms of interspecies communication and animal wisdom along with the unique messages that they continually bring into the space.

There is a sweet and familiar scent in the air, a scent that draws me into an old but familiar memory of my childhood in Montana with horses. It brings me back to the barren and sage-filled pastures that at a distance look like sheets of velvet folded over the rolling foothills of the Rockies. The old wooden cattle pens and barbed-wire fences that followed the contours of the land are now landmarks of the once fertile and working cattle ranches. Many years have passed and the ranches are gone, and so too am I, but the freshly laid hoofprints in the sand are evidence that the wild horses still roam this desolate land.

I continue to drift to a wonderful time in my life as a young girl when nothing of great importance existed for me except for horses. As if it were yesterday, I see myself walking alone down an old dirt road that followed the base of a small mountain, and I can still feel the unevenness of the ground and the swirls of dust that sting my face as the gusty wind blows across the open and desert-like land. Around the base of the bend is an old metal sign that prohibits shooting in the area, but is fully impaled and rotting with bullet holes making it hardly readable.

I continue to walk to the top of a large valley in great anticipation of catching a glimpse of the three resident horses grazing on the range. I can still smell the abundance of sage, and I can still feel the magnificence of their presence and never had I felt more free and at peace than I did with those three horses and nor could I have ever imagined that after all these years, they would still exist as such a profound and heartwarming part of me today.

The abrupt snorting of the horses quickly pulls me out of daydreaming, and it's now time to return to the barn as there are still a few minor details to prepare for nature's classroom and our guests will be arriving soon. As I begin to walk back I am overtaken by the sound of rumbling hooves coming up behind me and as I safely move out of their path I am highly amused by their playful demeanors as they joyfully gallop past me as if to question what has taken me so long to return. As they shuffle about I am happily greeted through their gentle nuzzling and snorting and they somehow seem to sense that today is another one of their magical days. In more ways than one, they always appear to be one step ahead of me in the preparation of our sacred teaching space, the land, for us and for those who are yet to come. As they come through and into their stalls there is a beautiful stillness that infiltrates the barn in which one cannot help but feel an overwhelming sense of calm, compassion, and inner peace when entering. There are no distractions, no disruptions, and no judgment; there is only the present moment where one is alone with one's self and their reflections in the four-legged mirrors that embrace the space around them.

Windsor is unusually quiet this morning and his typical strong and grounded leadership presence is somewhat laden in his unusual behavior. His natural bold and warrior-like presence is truly his most unique and expressive teaching trait in which so many are strangely intimidated but mysteriously drawn to him. He is highly respected in both his horse and human partnerships for his tremendous courage and perseverance in maintaining the highest integrity and relational dynamics of his herd and has often gone to great lengths to defend the instinctual values he upholds. His ability to beautifully dance within the dynamics of horse and human leadership roles has earned him my highest honor as a Guardian for the deepening and understanding of the horse human bond.

After offering him a small amount of hay he refuses to eat and continually shifts between sullen and restless behaviors. I do not get the sense that he is unwell and his behavior could be suggestive that he has possibly begun to connect with someone that has not yet arrived. I take a few moments to connect with him to try to decipher whether these feelings are actually his or mine when I am suddenly overwhelmed with sadness, my heart begins to feel heavy, and it is becoming increasingly harder to breathe. I close my eyes and continue to breathe further into the sensations in my body in an effort to understand what they are telling me. After a few moments, I intuitively know that this is not my pain and nor is it his. All that I can do for him in this moment is to acknowledge what he is taking on and honor that his deep sense of sadness and grief could possibly be reflective of someone who will soon be joining us today. In fully appreciating what he is carrying for someone else he begins to settle but continues to show his discord by occasionally pawing at his stall door. He is impatiently waiting and I am sensing that he knows whom he is waiting for.

The land, the horses, and nature's classroom are now prepared and fully embraced with compassion and open and willing hearts. The participants arrive and the opening circle is intentionally formed away from the horses, which always creates such great anticipation and wonder in the mystery of what lies behind those barn doors. We snuggle up in our chairs under our cozy fleece horse blankets and freshly brewed coffee. The unique blend of masculine and feminine energy the participants bring into the space today brings such a beautiful blend of personalities and expression to the group. I respectfully admire their apprehension amidst their childlike wonder of what is yet to be revealed. I equally appreciate the courage it takes to sit amongst those you do not know and to stir in the uncertainty of just how far the horses will want their individual journeys to go.

I briefly share my own personal life journey and speak to the magnificence of why horses are such powerful and perceptive teachers in bringing us closer to who we really are, through their innate ability to mirror or reflect our deepest feelings and hidden emotions. I move on to invite the first willing participant to share who they are and what has brought each of them to this self-discovery workshop with the horses today. Behind her shy and reserved demeanor she courageously steps forward and as she frequently glances down at her binder she quietly shares that she is lost and can no longer identify with who she is. A newly single mother of two beautiful young daughters, her anger and sense of betrayal run deep within her. Not only is she questioning the primary relationships in her life, she does not have a clear understanding of what she is going through and why. Standing alone in the rubble of her crumbled foundation she has finally heard the higher call for help but does not know where to turn or begin. For the first time in a long time and through coming here today, she feels a sense of hope that for once she may somehow be in control of her life. The life she had once known for 30 years had suddenly endured a turn of events that shattered all that she knew and filled her heart with anger, grief, and a deep sense of loss. Feeling hopelessly defeated she continued to spiral down into a dark and unfamiliar place where she could no longer identify with who she was.

As a close family friend, I have known Laura for many years and as she continues to share her story I feel a rush of sadness for her because her life has so quickly become unfamiliar to her. I quickly move through this feeling as I remind myself that she has come to the right place and to have faith in the horses and in the resilience of the human heart. Shortly after the birth of her second daughter, she endured the deepest form of betrayal by infidelity and the eventual breakdown of her marriage. This was un-expectantly followed by the death of her only sibling and older sister and not long thereafter the dissolution of her parent's 40-year marriage. Also, during this devastating time she had lost several beloved and long-time family pets.

In what seemed like an instant everything was gone, and shutting herself down in an effort to no longer have to deal with her challenges and huge loss, running as far away from herself as possible was her only way of coping. She yearned to be happy again but could not perceive any more loss in her life and she openly questioned why everything she loved was either dead or gone.

Morning with the horses

Heart connection

Jackie listening to Casper

Windsor's presence

As a facilitator I struggled to stay neutral and because of our close relationships, Windsor and I could not help but feel her pain. We had both known her so well through a time in her life when things were good and we knew what her normalcy was. Her loss was also a part of ours and our hearts helped carry her pain as she shared her story. My saving grace as a facilitator was my ability to shift back to neutral as my heart was also being guided by the horses in knowing that her presence here was a divine intervention, an intervention through faith in knowing that the horses would have the ability to reach her in a way that no one else could.

A box of multicolored crayons, colored pencils, and oil pastels are placed into the center of the circle and we begin our first exercise with the drawing of a Mandala. The Mandala begins with a large circle on a sheet of paper and each participant is asked to create and draw a representation of their journey through life within the circle; which most often reveals a reflection of both their inner and outer worlds. Drawn in pencil at the center of her Mandala circle is the head of a horse that is meticulously drawn with a beautiful flowing mane. There is no color, there are no nostrils nor are there eyes. There is barely a mouth and there is no expression or character drawn into the horse and looking at it through a facilitator's eye, it appears incomplete, lifeless, and empty.

She speaks of a past in which the horses were the center of her world, something in which she knew would always be in her heart and a significant part of her life. In large bold letters above the horse's head sits the word trust and is colored in red and is the most pronounced image on the page. Her voice softens and as she looks down at her picture she softly speaks of how everything in her life that she had come to trust was now gone and what she wanted more than anything was someone or something to trust in again. Below and to the right of the horse as if to represent the horse's body is the word strength but is less pronounced, colored in purple, and is bordered in a squiggly circle. She shares how she feels she has little strength left but yearns to find that part of herself that she once knew was strong.

As she continues to share her Mandala she struggles to speak as she points towards the bottom left hand side of the page where the word freedom is faintly written in blue and fading in color towards the end of the word. So trapped in a life of giving away her power to so many others, she no longer felt or understood what it was like to be free. There was a deeply profound honoring in witnessing the light of her resilience as she shared such heart-centered messages through the heaviness of her deepest pain. When we are given the opportunity to simply be still, we give ourselves the opportunity to distinguish and listen to the genuine voice of our higher self and only then will we come to trust that these are the messages we most often need to hear.

We then approach to enter the barn to meet the horses for the first time. As the rhythmical beats of the drums playing in the shamanic horse medicine music softly plays throughout the barn, the participants are mysteriously drawn into this magical space. Like an innate tribal call through the ancient teachings of the horse, I am always in awe to see these gifted healers shift into a deeper level of connection and healing when the music is playing in their presence. Each participant is instructed to simply meet the horses from a distance, no touching, no talking, just simple observations of their own thoughts and body reactions to each of the individual horses.

The group quietly enters the barn and Windsor's demeanor once again begins to change, and he becomes extremely agitated. He pins his ears back, repeatedly bangs his hoof against the stall door and continues to shake his head up and down. It is now becoming evident that his unusual behavior is clearly reflective for someone in this group. Having a past significant relationship with Windsor and not having seen him in a few years, Laura's direct avoidance of him was highly observable to me as she moved away from him and intentionally went on to see the others. He followed her every move, waited for her to make eye contact, and in sensing her intention to avoid him he continued in his agitation until it was blatantly obvious that he was doing everything he could to reach her.

We left the barn after 15 minutes to move back outside to review the exercise along with each of their experiences. I felt such deep compassion for him as I intuitively knew in that moment that he not only remembered who she was and the relationship they shared in the past but he was desperately trying to reach her. He was frustrated at his failed attempts to connect with her, but I knew in my heart that if his typical consistent and determined behavior as a leader was to prevail, his opportunity to reach her was sure to come again. As the morning progressed, I was trusted that the process was unfolding exactly as it needed to and also in the herd's ability to manifest exactly the right teaching moment for him.

We moved on to do another exercise that involves working with the multiple layers of energy that emanate from the physical body to become more respectful of the personal space for both horses and humans. Because we all have these multiple and fluctuating layers of energy based on how an individual person or horse is feeling, we can be quite successful in finding them once we become more observant of the horse's body language as we are moving into and through the layers. In this type of energy work we often ask the participants to put their arms out to the side, palms facing forward, as this is where most will begin to feel the energy. Windsor's large body mass and grounded presence makes him the perfect teacher for this type of energy work and with a grass-covered base in the round pen he thoroughly enjoys the activity as he is simply allowed to graze during the process.

Windsor is brought into the round pen and is released so that he now has the freedom to be at liberty throughout the exercise. He graciously entertains us with his grazing while the first two participants easily move through the exercise and continues to do so while Laura is preparing to go next. As we approach to open the gate to allow her to enter the pen, Windsor suddenly stops eating and abruptly raises his head and stands at attention in a statue like posture. He begins to watch her intensely and continues to do so as she positions herself away from him, let's her hands open to the horse, and begins the exercise by walking towards him. Unlike how most would approach and move through this exercise she surprises me by very abruptly walking right up into his personal space and stops less than a foot away from his body.

"I don't feel anything," she softly says as she disappointingly stares into the ground.

Windsor begins to aggressively paw at the ground but freely chooses not to move away from her.

"Ok," I replied. "Let's just slowly begin to back away from him so that we can move out of his personal space and perhaps move towards him again a little slower this time or just slowly begin to move around him to see if you can get a sense of where you might begin to feel something in your hands or in your body."

She backs out of his space, opens her hands, and once again abruptly walks right back up into his personal space and stands facing the left side of his body. He continues to watch her intensely and this time she says nothing but stands silently beside him and continues to stare at the ground. In the uncertainty of what may be unfolding I remain silent as they both continue to stand motionless for a few moments until once again Windsor begins to paw at the ground but much more aggressively this time. It was clear to me that he was now asking for his opportunity to change the course of the exercise and to move into a deeper level of connection and resonance with Laura. In trusting that this masterful teacher was being guided to offer what she truly needed to move forward, I respectfully allow him to continue.

The intensity of their embrace feels somewhat like a stand-off and was nothing quite like I had ever seen him do before. It was clearly evident that she had built a shield of armor that was effectively protecting her from feeling anything that was going on around her but sadly leaving her so shut down and disconnected from her body that as a result it was making it very difficult for Windsor to reach her. Typically when a participant opens their hands in this exercise they usually experience a tingling or warming sensation in their palms or somewhere in the front of their body that makes them aware that they are feeling some degree of energetic activity. For Laura, nothing of the sort existed and nor she could she even begin to imagine that it could.

As if all time were standing still, there was nothing I could say to her in this moment other than to continue to hold the space for what was beginning to happen. As she raises her head to look at him Windsor suddenly stops pawing at the ground and embraced in one of the most profound heart-to-heart connections that I have ever witnessed, he continues to allow her experience to unfold. Like counting the seconds that elapse between thunder and lightning we all compassionately embraced in the stillness of the anticipation for some beautiful eruption of something that had long been brewing. He was so highly attuned to the deep emotional storm within her that the sharp focus of his eye into hers could only have been what we often describe as looking into the soul of another living being. The eyes are said to be the window to the soul and only have I on very few occasions seen and felt such an intensity of soulful exchange from another living being and only through the eyes of a horse. Although this deep and sacred spiritual experience is seen through the eyes it is profoundly felt in tremendous depth through the heart. There was a much deeper level of love, compassion, and connection that was needed for Laura in this moment in order for her to feel safe enough to trust in what her heart wanted her to do. There was nothing more magical in this moment for us than to witness this union of two beautiful and familiar souls through the purity of the heart's resonance.

Unlike anything she had ever experienced before, she suddenly began to feel her body becoming extremely heavy like a gravitational pull through her feet to the earth. She began to feel an intensity of energy or pressure slowly building up through her spine, crossing upwards and over the front of her body, and then up around her throat. In this exact moment of intensity Windsor suddenly turned and gently placed his head on her chest. With his forehead lying over her heart and his muzzle softly resting in her hands, she finally began to cry. Feeling extremely vulnerable and emotionally exposed and in not understanding what was now happening to her she quickly attempted to stop herself but Windsor refused to lift his head from her heart.

"Laura?" I softly said in a compassionate voice. "It's okay to cry. He wants you to cry."

It was her opportunity to resist what was happening to her and to avoid listening to what her heart truly wanted to reveal, but it was Windsor's perseverance and powerful grounded presence in holding a non-judgmental and compassionate space that allowed her to feel emotionally safe enough to continue. It often can be difficult and confusing to fully understand what is happening to us when our hearts begin to take the lead and our logical minds cannot always process what is happening in our bodies until we have the opportunity to understand how it so wonderfully speaks to us. This was such a beautiful witnessing of the powerful inner battle that so often occurs between the compassionate heart and the logical mind and was truly an amazing display of how powerful these two interconnected intelligence centers can work apart only then to come together to integrate the learning for the higher purpose of healing and soul growth.

As the heavy and painful sensations continued to travel up her spine this was her moment of truth, and she was now facing the rawness of her pain. Windsor remained at her heart as she continued to cry and his previous saddened and frustrated demeanor had now transformed to one of love and compassion and there was something through him in this moment that now felt so familiar to her.

When the time was right I quietly asked, "Laura, what are you experiencing in your body now?"

As she continued to cry, she softly whispered, "I feel like I'm having a homecoming."

Her deep sense of comfort and peace was truly a call for her to come home, not only through her familiarity to him but to an aspect of herself that was free from the circumstances in which she felt had so unjustly defined who she had become. As she continued to cry the pain subsided and her body began to feel lighter. Standing face to face with an old friend, she no longer felt alone and for the first time in a long time she now knew she was going to be okay. He had brought her back to a familiar place within herself in which to begin a new journey, a journey where she could now trust in herself to be in control of her own life, to find the strength to face her challenges, and to experience the freedom to love herself in the process. When we are able to fully acknowledge our suffering and free ourselves from the confines of our pain through the intelligence of another species it is truly one of the highest acts of unconditional love. Emotionally and physically drained she raised her hand and began to softly stroke his neck. As she quietly thanked him no words could define the depth of her experience, and she would now be forever grateful for his deep compassion and for the impact his hoofprints will forever leave on her heart.

The day has come to an end and everyone is gone. The horses are quietly resting and judging by the occasional nodding of his head Windsor appears peaceful but exhausted. As I raise my hand to stroke his forehead he acknowledges my touch and gently nudges me with his nose. A true warrior of the heart, I am truly touched by his willingness and courage in taking on such a deep emotional battle in his role as teacher today when he is always offered the choice to simply walk away. His brilliance and determination in reaching out to a beautiful soul so deeply lost in her pain is a true testament to the emotional heroism we so often witness within the realm of our healing partnerships with horses.

We are guided on our journey through life through the intelligence and profound experiences of the heart, and we can always trust that our hearts will remember who we are. This gifted and higher intelligence of the heart works in perfect unison and in harmony with the body and soul and when in the presence of a horse can never be ignored. When we are lost or simply seeking to find more, the horses will always hear our call and will gently guide us on our way back to the place in our hearts that authentically recognizes the road to the journey home. One cannot imagine the power and brilliance that lies within the wisdom of the horse until one has the opportunity to experience such a profound and impactful interaction. When we are embraced within the space of a horse something deep within us begins to change, and we no longer fear our greatest weakness in the burdens we carry but we begin to find the wisdom and unlimited possibilities within ourselves that are yet to be discovered.

The gateway to our soul can be found through the path of the horse as the wisdom and intelligence in everything you need to know lies in their ability to bring the hidden or over-protected aspects of ourselves into the light of our awareness. Once opened to our awareness only then can we begin the process of personal transformation, inner growth, and healing. This is truly one of the most precious and authentic gifts that we can receive from another living being. The journey to our hearts through the magical and mystical teachings of horse medicine is where we as humans can reunite with the purity and essence of who we are and there is no other more loving, gentle, and compassion, way than that through the way of the horse.

I will be forever grateful to the horses for continuing to walk beside me as I continue on this journey into the realm of healing and personal growth. I never would have imagined in my earlier years that my life passion would evolve and unfold to the level that it has today through working this way with horses. As a teenage girl the stable was my most trusted haven for emotional support and stability and my relationships with the horses were truly my most respected, trustworthy, and highly regarded friendships. Only through my own personal healing work with the horses have I really come to more fully understand the nature and impact that these fascinating animals have in the healing of the human spirit.

As a life coach who has integrated the FEEL horse work into my practice, I am truly honored and deeply inspired time and time again by the witnessing of the profound and incredible life-changing moments of others and also in exploring the exciting opportunities for the unlimited and untapped potential for human expansion, healing, and growth through horses. As so many will attest to, their most heartwarming and memorable experiences created through the spirit of the horse medicine teachings are so deeply rooted within their soul that they can never be forgotten, but more amazingly they are so easily recalled as the gentle nudge that keeps us moving in our desired direction.

Eighteen years ago, Windsor left his Northern Alberta home for mine in Ontario in light of my high expectations for him in becoming my next dressage prospect. There was something very intriguing about the qualities of this narrow-chested, oddly colored, and wild little horse that somehow reflected the qualities that I so deeply wanted to preserve about my own nature. After all these years I have come to the final conclusion that we never mastered the art of cantering. The mere thought of a braided mane, a pristine appearance, and fancy show tack simply made him cringe but his witty, mischievous, and curious nature captivated my heart in so many wonderful and awe-inspiring ways. It was through the lightness and comedy of our tug-o-war relationship in wanting a show horse versus his desire to be a world explorer that he eventually found a way to challenge my beliefs about the way in which I relate to horses and to guide me into a whole new world of healing and authentic relationship with horses.

Some of our most precious gifts are those that we give ourselves through challenging our own beliefs about how we show up in our lives or present ourselves to others. One of the greatest and priceless pleasures that I have discovered in this work is to know that for all those unwanted, old, broken, abused, or retired horses, there is now a much grander purpose for their lives than we are often led to believe. I am deeply grateful to Windsor in presenting the challenge around my own patterns and behaviors with horses and in his ability to help me rewrite new belief systems that oddly led me to becoming the new owner of a beautiful white horse called Casper, unknowingly accompanied by a serious and painful eye condition that causes blindness in horses. Just a few short months after acquiring him his condition gradually began to claim the vision in his left eye and at this time an unknown degree of vision loss in his right eye. Never had I dealt with this condition in a horse and during the course of my first few months with him I regretfully felt I had made a huge mistake in taking ownership of him and could not perceive how I was going to manage a vision-impaired horse.

I sense now that many wonder what purpose this partially blind horse Casper has had in my life these past three years and if only I could begin to share the richness and value in which he has, it would be an incredible story on its own. From what I have witnessed on his journey into darkness, the survival of a horse of this nature would be highly unlikely in the wild and perhaps equally as unlikely in our human world. One might expect for him to be unpredictable and dangerous to handle as his vision deteriorates, but in my experience this couldn't be further from the truth based on my willingness to learn through a deeper and more subtle language of such a horse. My ability to offer him a grounded and safe path in which to follow is greatly in part due to his wisdom in teaching me to reflect what he needs to feel safe by staying grounded, attuned to my inner awareness, and aware of my emotional states as much as I humanly can. It is he who has taught me; I have simply been the receptive, willing, and open-minded student.

He is driven to survive in a world that may not fully understand his viability through such an impairment. He teaches us more about ourselves so that we can begin to discover the brilliance in what we so often perceive as less than perfect or not enough. His unique gifts and heightened awareness of other senses not ordinarily developed holds such great potential and capacity for a new way of understanding our relationships with others and in learning the art of non-verbal communication. We have courageously walked this journey together in light of our struggles. Through his own evolution of healing and growth he has so elegantly evolved into one of our most masterful and compassionate healers. His extraordinary ability to perceive in others what were once aspects of his old but familiar world has now become his greatest passage for developing courage, confidence, trust, and self-esteem in others.

I spend my days feeling blessed and grateful for the opportunity to spend my life in the presence of such masterful teachers. As the horses never fail to show me new possibilities for healing and growth, I continue to admire the way in which they repeatedly chose to step into each new challenge presented before them. I continue to spend endless hours simply sitting and reflecting with my horses. Stepping out of the reality of my everyday life and into the way of the horse can only be described as nothing less than extraordinary and magical. My childhood dream of spending my life with horses in a way that brings greater purpose and passion to the lives of both horses and humans has evolved far beyond my expectations. As I continue to walk my path with horses, I look forward to dreaming in the unlimited possibilities and opportunities to freelance, travel, and to write about my experiences as I take this work out to humans and horses around the world.

It's been more than 35 years since I've been gone from the time these old memories were made and once again I am reunited with this long and winding road that brings me back to the base of that old mountain. Like stepping back in time, that old metal sign is still impaled with bullet holes and very little about the valley has changed. Sage still covers the barren land, the old farmhouse in the distance still stands, but sadly there are no longer hoof prints in the sand. To whomever they were or to whomever they belonged, the horses of yesterday will forever live on through the instinctual species wisdom and heart-centered interactions of the incredibly gifted and compassionate horse teachers of today. May our presence always be graced and our hearts always be touched by the magnificence and captivating beauty of this most majestic and magnificent being that we have all come to know today as the horse.

Jackie Ladouceur

Jackie Ladouceur, a Certified FEEL Practitioner, was born with an innate passion for horses and first realized her passion as a young girl being raised in Butte, Montana. After moving to Ontario in her early teens she spent many years learning about horses in the Canadian Pony Club and was an avid competitor on the hunter and dressage show circuits. She continues to be a supporter of natural dressage and horsemanship methods and is deeply passionate and dedicated to the fields of FEEL (Facilitated Equine Experiential Learning) and life coaching.

In her chosen career fields as a registered veterinary technician and primary care paramedic she is equally passionate about helping and healing both animals and humans. After graduating as a Stress and Wellness Consultant with the Canadian Institute of Stress, Hans Selye Foundation, Jackie went on to study and graduate from Erickson College, Vancouver, B.C. as an Erickson Certified Life Coach.

She is the founder of Fields of Wisdom, an organization dedicated to transforming the lives of people through horses, where she currently integrates the FEEL horse work with her life coaching sessions and workshops as well as in her energy work as a Reiki Master. She is grateful to be a founding member of the FEEL Honoring the Horse committee in which she dedicates her time as an advocate for the voice of the horse in the FEEL work.

For more information on Jackie and Fields of Wisdom, please visit: www.fieldsofwisdom.com

CHAPTER 2

Know Thyself, Be True

By Jennifer Schramm

Since I can remember I have dreamed of a life with horses. Growing up in a suburb of southern Ontario, I lived a mere half-hour drive from the stable where I started taking riding lessons at the age of 5 and boarded my first horse, Easy. Horses defined my childhood. My first word as a baby was "horsey." I began riding as soon as I could sit on my grandpa's lap while he sat astride the horse. Horses soon began occupying my thoughts during the day and my dreams at night.

As a little girl, my favourite pastimes were washing horse brushes, jumping my dog as though she were a horse, and jumping as though I were a horse, always looking for the perfect distance. I loved tacking up my horse and riding her cross-country. Together we'd travel across streams and rivers, hack in the woods, and gallop through snow banks. After school, I would focus my energy exclusively on horse-related activities. Riding lessons. Horse camp. Hanging out at my grandpa's farm. Reading horse novels. Watching *My Little Pony*. Reading books about different breeds. Talking about horses. (Do you get the picture?) I loved brushing and petting horses, and feeding them apples and carrots. By the time I was a teenager, I was thoroughly horse obsessed.

Towards the end of high school, when I began contemplating potential careers, I wanted to make sure of two things. First, I wanted to spend all day with horses. Second, I wanted to earn a lot of money.

Being a veterinarian seemed like the perfect fit. The only trouble was I couldn't see or be near blood without fainting, quickly ruling out that option. I then thought about becoming a professional show jumper. Despite the many hours I'd spent on horseback as well as taking formal riding lessons, I knew I wasn't talented enough as an equestrian to compete, nor did I have the guts to take on those huge jumps. A career with horses began to seem increasingly unlikely. To top it all off, I felt a lack of support in the horse community. Everyone told me that horses were a "lose money" sport, and that I would never be able to make a living working with them.

No longer able to see myself having a fruitful career with horses, I stopped believing it was possible to have a horse of my own, let alone run a horse business. Instead, I focused on a new goal: partying. After graduating with a university degree in psychology, I spent the next 10 years working in the corporate world and having a good time. Horses barely entered my life, except for the occasional trail ride when I went on vacation. Even though I didn't have the life with horses I'd always dreamed of, at least I could say I was successful, developing my career as a business woman and moving up the corporate ladder. All that mattered to me during that time was getting people to like me, being successful, and trying to fit in. But worrying so much about everyone else's opinions all my life was finally catching up with me.

What no one knew was that I had been secretly fighting an eating disorder since I was 16 years old, two years after my beloved horse, Thumbs Up, had died, and one year after I had stopped riding altogether. Losing Thumbs Up had devastated me. Not having a focus, I had turned my attention to boys, partying, alcohol, and drugs, becoming the quintessential party girl. It was easy to pull off, because everyone in my peer group was doing the exact same thing. On top of all that partying, I had a new obsession: getting thin. What had started as a casual preoccupation with my weight in high school became an out-of-control eating disorder when I went away to university to study psychology, of all things. I was trapped in a cycle of over-exercising at the gym, taking three-dozen laxatives a day, binging, and restricting my food intake. I also wasn't spending any time with horses. My thoughts were consumed with calorie counting and my next meal. I was malnourished, chronically dehydrated, and couldn't think straight. Many times I ended up fainting in the shower. My anxiety was constant and debilitating, and I suffered from insomnia. In spite of growing ever skinnier, I felt completely insecure.

Looking back over my life, it's now obvious and not the least bit coincidental that the further away I'd been from horses, the less connected I had felt to myself, and the sicker I'd become. While living the party girl lifestyle around the world, I had hidden my eating disorder from everyone, including myself. In my early twenties, after university, travelling, and working around the world, I ended up accepting a job in Toronto and living with my parents. My eating disorder was out of control. I had clearly hit rock bottom and needed help.

First, I visited a family physician. Very quickly, I realized that the conventional medical approach would fail to help me. The physician was only interested in prescribing drugs to treat my symptoms, drugs that made me so ill that I decided never to take another pill again. My mom, being an advocate of alternative therapy, insisted that I see a medical intuitive instead. I agreed, as I was always one for trying something out of the box and different. Atherton, the medical intuitive, impressed me. She was dressed smart, had short, stylish red hair, and was professional in her demeanor. During our first meeting, Atherton was blunt: She said I was lucky to be alive. Her words made me look honestly, for the first time, at what I had been doing to myself. Around the same time, I had started riding my grandpa's horse Classy, a chestnut thoroughbred off the track. I spent as many as five or six days a week riding her over the course of a year. And without any additional treatment, besides seeing Atherton, my eating disorder gradually started to improve. I started feeling more connected to myself and a little more at peace.

Without realizing it, my healing journey with horses had begun. When I was with Classy, I forgot about my negative self-talk and my body image and eating issues. I was more committed to spending time with Classy and caring for her. While I was with her, most of my destructive patterns fell off the radar. Classy gave me a new focus and something to look forward to.

As part of the healing process, Atherton told me that I needed to reconnect with my passions, going so far as to suggest that I needed to work in a career I actually felt passionate about. Well, that was an entirely foreign concept to me! Years ago, when I had discovered that horses were not going to be part of my dream life, my goal had become earning recognition and making a good income. And here she was saying that I needed to focus on my passions once more.

With this little healing seed planted in 2001, my brain began to churn. I wondered how I could incorporate horses into my life again. I had always loved how I felt around horses—calm and warm inside. And I preferred to groom and ride them on the flat more than anything else. Maybe there was a way to live my dream after all.

While working as a sales trainer in Vancouver, continuing to heal from the eating disorder, I found myself contemplating my life and career after work one day. I decided to take Atherton's suggestion more seriously. So I asked myself, *What career can I do that involves horses?* Strangely enough, that little healing seed began to sprout when I quit my sales job and became a horse insurance broker. Taking that risk reignited my belief that I could have a career with horses. Realizing that I also wanted to help people who struggled with eating disorders, I decided to pursue a counseling degree in Vancouver.

While still in school, I was introduced to healing with horses by a friend who invited me to an evening seminar being given by Barbara Rector, a pioneer in this field. Listening to Barbara talk about healing with horses, I felt inspired. I was in heaven! *This is my calling*, I thought. I didn't know how I was going to make it a reality, but I said to myself, *One day I am going to do this!* Barbara Rector's way of working with horses was not traditional, but a new way of relating to them, where people and horses were in a therapeutic relationship together, and I was excited to learn more about it.

My next therapeutic interaction with horses took place at the beginning of my counseling career almost a decade ago, when I was flown out for a site visit to an eating disorder recovery centre in Arizona. Seeing their equine-assisted program left me feeling intrigued: I couldn't believe that it was possible to marry these two seemingly unrelated passions. I became captivated with the idea of pursuing this training. Back in Toronto, I couldn't stop talking with colleagues and clients about the profound healing I'd witnessed thanks to the horses.

Many years passed, and I finally began researching different programs that would allow me to bridge my counseling experience with this equine-assisted work. I took a workshop to learn more about this experiential work at Horse Spirit Connections. I wanted to try it for myself before becoming certified. I attended a two-day workshop called Discover Your Inner Wisdom. The logical side of me remained slightly skeptical. Was this horse work a legitimate healing modality or simply another fad? I decided to stay open to the experience. Maybe the horses could teach me something about myself.

I showed up at the farm early in the morning to meet the facilitators and five participants. Right away, I felt thrown off by the shamanistic flavour of the meeting room, the sweat lodge outside, and the buffalo head mounted on the wall. It all seemed too New Agey for my liking. What was I doing here? My senses were on high alert, and I began judging the facilitators' every move. As we introduced ourselves, I learned that I was the only one with horse experience and that one lady was absolutely terrified of horses. I started thinking that maybe this work would only benefit people without horse experience. The methods didn't seem like they'd work for me, because it felt too basic to be learning about horses like a beginner. I knew how to lead a horse. I knew how to be with a horse. I knew what horses were capable of. Or so I thought.

That's when I met Paris. We did an exercise called Reflective Round Pen. When it was my turn, I announced that my intention was to get into a relationship with a man. I was ready to find a boyfriend. I was tired of being single! As Andre, my facilitator, led me through a body scan, I noticed the butterflies in my stomach and some serious shoulder pain. Andre asked me how intense my pain was on a scale of one to ten. I said "Seven." He then asked me whether my shoulders had a message for me. Immediately, I heard the words "Let go." Then he told me to turn towards Paris, my partner horse, and state my heart's desire for the session, which was to let go of what was holding me back from being in a relationship.

I entered the round pen, confident and ready to connect with Paris. As I walked up to her, inching my way towards her, she kept moving farther and farther away. Now, all my shame and insecurities began to surface. *Oh my God, what are people going to think? I'm the only person here with horse experience, and I can't get the horse to come to me or connect with me.* In fact, Paris seemed repulsed by me. I kept trying to get close to her, but it wasn't working. I felt more stupid with every passing moment. My insides were in a knot. I felt so embarrassed and ashamed that I couldn't get this horse to like me. Then, something inside me urged me to simply pause. And as I paused, sitting with all the discomfort, I received an insight.

What Paris was showing me was, alarmingly, a long-held pattern: I was always trying to get people to like me. Not only was this a huge insight into my desire to find a man, it was also something I did with all the people in my life. I wanted everyone to like me and to instantly connect with me. Paris taught me that I didn't have to connect with everyone. I certainly didn't like everyone I met, so why did everyone have to like me?

I began to process feelings that had been running my life for years. I had been chasing men that weren't right for me. I had been doing everything to get them to like me when they clearly weren't interested. I was wasting time going after things that didn't feel right and wallowing in misery about being constantly rejected rather than looking for connections that did feel good and that did work. I could see this pattern not only with men but also with my clients, my family, my friends, and my colleagues. My actions were about doing things to get people to like me rather than being true to myself and just being me.

Paris' response of walking away from me and not connecting to me also made me realize that it didn't matter what people thought about me. It didn't matter if I was the horse expert and couldn't connect with a horse. Not always connecting, and feeling vulnerable about it, was a natural part of life. I learned that vulnerability was the source of my power. Everyone's power, in fact. I didn't have to be perfect at everything. Being imperfect —asking for help, not feeling a connection, or admitting weakness—was what made me human. It was hard for me to wrap my head around this at first, because it was the opposite of what I, and most of us, were taught to believe: that vulnerability is a weakness, not a strength. But I didn't have to maintain a façade any longer. I left the session with a huge weight lifted off my shoulders. Who would have thought a sweet black mare named Paris would share such a profound message with me, one that would truly begin to transform my life?

On the second day of the workshop, I partnered with Thor, a stunning black Percheron gelding. My new intention was to explore a way of being that would attract a relationship. I entered the round pen alone, and sat on a chair in the middle of the pen. I focused on my own feelings, not on what Thor was doing. I got up and walked around when I felt like it, and I didn't try to have a connection with him. I just breathed. Thor became interested in my every move and even came up to me on several occasions throughout the session. When I sat down in the centre of the round pen, he rested his head on my heart. All I had to do was breathe and be me.

I have transferred these lessons to all areas of my life. I developed a new awareness at the cellular level, so profound that I could feel it in my bones. I felt lighter, at peace, calm, and like I had more space in my mind. I stopped being overly nice and accommodating with clients. I stopped trying to get every man to like me and started asking myself what was important to me, what felt good regardless of what other people were saying or doing. What others did was really none of my business.

That weekend, I learned so much about my inner patterns and my attachment to wanting people to like me. I was sold on equine-assisted learning and decided to take the FEEL Certification Program so that I would be able to share this work with others. But I had no horse, and I had no idea how a business like this would come to be. But I trusted that it would. And it did.

Over the span of a year, I worked with individual clients and held a few equine-assisted learning workshops at Horse Spirit Connections, but I was still primarily working with clients in my counseling/coaching practice in the city. I wanted to grow my work with horses, so I started brainstorming. I had almost 10 years of counseling and coaching experience and a lifetime of horse experience which gave me credibility. Coincidentally, my friend had just inherited a farm. When I mentioned wanting to have my own equine-assisted learning centre, she said that I could use her 10-stall barn for my business. I couldn't believe it! I then asked for guidance from the universe, a sign that I was on the right path. As luck would have it, only a couple of days later, I received an email from my friend Shona telling me about a horse that needed a home. That's how my first horse, a bay mare named Astella, joined the healing herd. Just over a month later, I had five horses and Unbridled Experiences was born.

Now, less than two years later, I am a FEEL Practitioner running my own FEEL (Facilitated Equine Experiential Learning) centre. Never in my wildest dreams did I think I would have a FEEL centre and that I could be in a two-way relationship with horses where we were both learning and healing together. When I wake up in the morning and greet my herd, I feel a sense of joy and peace as we connect. As I prepare for workshops, I feel so grateful that I get to love what I do and at the same time help people and horses. I get to see people's lives change. As a little girl learning to ride, I never imagined that these brilliant and magnificent beings would become an integral part of my healing journey and my life's purpose.

When I was first introduced to equine therapy, I wasn't living life for me. I was attached to perfecting outer appearances and trying to fix other people. I was attracted to the qualities in others that I hadn't yet developed in myself, like self-acceptance and faith and confidence in my true nature. My intimate relationships and friendships were full of drama and dysfunction. By focusing on inner healing and learning to identify unhealthy patterns in myself, I am now able to be fully present more often. My relationships are deeper and more satisfying. Material possessions no longer define who I am. Once I started living life for me, the dream I had abandoned years ago took on a life of its own and flourished. I feel connected to my passion. Even more importantly, I feel reconnected to myself. It was a good thing that I ignored my inner skeptic and allowed myself to experience the depth of this amazing, magical work.

I continue to be amazed and grateful that I built my own FEEL centre, where people can come to learn about themselves, how they show up in the world, and how they can become more congruent with their true natures. After 37 years of being around horses, I continue to learn something new from them every day. I am embracing the light and the dark traits, both my own and those of the horses. Here are a few more stories from clients who also experienced a reconnection with themselves through FEEL work.

Jennifer horsing around as a young girl

Jennifer and her first horse, Easy

Jennifer at a horse show with her pony, Thumbs Up

Jennifer and Rosa at Horse Spirit Connections

Rosa. Boundaries: Staying Grounded in Your Own Truth

It was a hot summer day early in my career when I met Melissa, one of my first FEEL clients. Melissa was a slim, gentle woman in her mid-40s. She had been referred to me through a mutual colleague. Ten years ago, she told me, she had hated nature. She had wanted the world to be covered in concrete and for people to have no hair. The thought of animals and bugs and grass and trees had irritated her. However, after a complete life transformation that saw her leave an unfulfilling corporate career and a 17-year marriage, Melissa had reconnected to another side of herself. She learned that nature inspired her and made her feel peaceful. She was developing a new relationship with the natural world. Although Melissa had very little experience with horses and animals in general, she was open to what they could teach her.

I asked Melissa what her intention was for the session. She said she was open, curious, and wanted to gain more awareness about herself. Here's how it showed up with the horses.

With her intention set, we made our way up to the barn, where we began with an exercise called Meet the Herd. All six-herd members were in their stalls inside the barn, and Melissa was going to have the chance to meet and connect with them. While merely observing the horses in silence and without touching, she was to note her impressions using all her senses and her body awareness: colours, emotions, words, sounds, and so on. I asked her to pay attention to her body, her thoughts, and her inner knowing as she met with each horse. Then I asked her to choose a horse that she most resonated with, that she felt was calling to work with her and had wisdom to offer her today.

As Melissa started the exercise, I noticed that she was moving quickly from horse to horse. But as time went on, I saw her relaxing and spending more time with each horse. When I asked her which horse she wanted to work with, Melissa told me that she had most resonated with Rosa and wanted to work with her. When I asked why, she said that she appreciated Rosa's gentleness, beauty, and soft way.

I knew Rosa well. She was a stunningly beautiful grey mare who could at the same time be quite a bully. She wanted what she wanted and wasn't afraid to assert her strength. Indeed, she had even chosen her job as a healing horse. Years ago, Rosa had been a riding horse and decided that she didn't want to be ridden anymore. Her owner didn't know what to do and wanted answers. She decided to call an animal intuitive, who told her that Rosa wanted to be a healing horse. Her owner, having no clue what that even meant, Googled "healing horses" and found Horse Spirit Connections, where Rosa now has a forever home. Melissa was intrigued by this story.

Our next stop was the round pen. I haltered Rosa and began walking the hundred metres towards the round pen. As we approached, Rosa stopped dead in her tracks, planted her feet, and didn't want to move any farther. In my head, I thought to myself, *Oh shit, how am I going to explain this? What kind of horsewoman am I? I can't even get this horse into the round pen.* Then I took a deep breath and trusted that there was a message in this for Melissa. I asked her whether this was a usual occurrence for her. She said yes, that it brought up a feeling of frustration and that she just wanted to get on with it.

I asked Melissa to do an exercise where she would lead Rosa around the arena from the pylon at point A to the pylon at point B. I passed the lead rope to Melissa, and Rosa began dragging her all over the arena. Melissa was simply going along with it. She was allowing Rosa to lead her. It appeared as though Rosa had taken over and that Melissa didn't have a say in anything that was going on.

I walked over to them and took the lead rope from Melissa, asking her whether this reminded her of anything in her life. She said yes. She was allowing herself to get swayed by what everyone else wanted her to do. She didn't feel grounded or rooted in herself and was being pulled all over the place by her kids, her ex-husband, her parents, her clients. She was trying to be everything for everyone and was forgetting about herself in the process.

Rosa was being pushy and a little jumpy, so I asked Melissa to step aside while I held Rosa with my feet firmly on the ground. I stood there, rooted and grounded. Rosa could do whatever she wanted. She could jitter and move around, but I wasn't going anywhere. I was standing still, feet firmly planted. Eventually, Rosa settled and stood right beside me.

What Melissa realized was that she was getting hooked into everyone else's drama and life. She was allowing other people's beliefs, behaviours, and ideas to distract her from herself. She was buying into their stuff, had no boundaries, and felt pulled in all directions.

Melissa learned from Rosa that she could be grounded and rooted in herself regardless of what other people were doing. It was okay for them to be uncomfortable with their feelings, and it was okay for her to stand there like a rock while they had their own experience instead of feeding into it or trying everything in her power to make them comfortable at her expense. This was a huge "Aha!" for Melissa.

A year after her session, Melissa told me how this experience with Rosa had transformed her life. Rosa had taught her the power of being true to herself. She was different in her relationships. She was okay with saying no to her kids, and she became comfortable with the discomfort of their discontent. She was able to share more of her true self with her parents and became confident in her choices, even though her parents had other ideas for her. She was okay about saying no to people who weren't her ideal clients and drained her energy. She learned to be true to herself and confident in her actions, even if people didn't agree or had a negative reaction to her truth.

Thanks to Rosa, Melissa learned the power of being true to herself regardless of what other people around her were saying or doing.

Thor. Emotional Congruency: Getting Real

At the beginning of my career, I used to do a lot of sessions at Horse Spirit Connections. Wendy and Andre, who run the business, were generous enough to let me use their facility. One of their healing horses is a beautiful black Percheron gelding named Thor. He is a gentle giant full of wisdom and grace. He has the softest heart, the wisest eyes, and the gentlest soul. Having said that, he was also a master teacher who always perfectly mirrored whatever needed to be reflected.

One morning, my client Jack arrived at the farm. He was a handsome 21-year-old actor who was working on overcoming an eating disorder and low self-esteem. He had been a victim of the entertainment industry, where people had criticized him about his body, his looks, his voice, and his vibe, among other things. Jack was very sensitive from enduring many years of criticism, judgment, and rejection. He had been a teen model and a television star. Now, he was working to come to peace with his experiences so that acting could be a fun, joyous, and healthy career again.

Jack deeply loved animals and was very interested in working with the horses. Looking like a typical movie star, he arrived in his blue sports car, shades on, casually dressed with a cool vibe.

The horses were already out in the field, so Jack and I joined them. We first did a grounding exercise where Jack connected with his body, mind, spirit, and breath. Then I invited him to connect with the six horses that were out in the field without touching or talking to them and to choose the horse that he felt most drawn to or called by. As he moved through the field connecting with all the horses, Thor showed interest. He was very engaged in the connection with Jack.

"I'd like to work with this big guy," Jack said.

I asked him why he felt drawn to Thor, and he replied, "He's big, a little intimidating, and it seems like it may be a challenge."

I walked Thor to the round pen. He sniffed around, walking in his very slow, nonchalant way, exploring the space until he eventually came to a halt. Thor stood still and looked at me, giving me the cue that he was ready to work with Jack. Jack made his way into the centre of the round pen, where he stated his intention to Thor. His intention: healing and confidence.

I began to notice Thor's behavior right away. He was standing against the side of the round pen. His ears were back and he kicked his back legs out a couple of times very slowly, like cow kicks, He looked irritated and angry. This was a behaviour I had not seen in Thor before.

I asked Jack what was going on inside him. From my view, he was standing there in the pen, body a little tense, and a concerned look on his face.

"I am trying to control him with my energy," he said. "He is reminding me of my dad, who is so powerful, and I am trying to control him with my energy. I am feeling really angry with my dad and the way I have been treated and bullied all my life. This is the way I relate to people when I feel threatened."

Jack told me that he had always felt nonverbally threatened by people that were bigger than him and had authority over him. He had begun taking steroids in his teens and working out regularly at the gym. His body grew in size, and he felt more powerful. At the time, he said he thought "these guys can't hurt me anymore because I am bigger." He believed that the bigger he was, the safer he would feel. Yet, inside he was hurting. He felt like a child and was soft and scared. He was trying to portray to Thor that he was bigger than him, and he was using his energy to give Thor the impression that he was bigger and stronger. Except his tactic wasn't working. Thor was reflecting it right back to him, and the fear inside Jack didn't subside. It only escalated and made him angrier.

Thor was reflecting back to Jack exactly what Jack was giving out energetically. It was truly amazing to witness. Jack began to cry. As he continued to share his feelings, to get clear on his pattern and become more real and vulnerable, Thor relaxed and untensed his body. Jack was realizing what he had been doing. He had been fighting his fear by trying to appear stronger and bigger, but it wasn't working in his real life and it wasn't working with Thor. He was scared and vulnerable beneath his tough exterior.

As Jack became more vulnerable and authentic with what he was feeling, Thor gently and slowly walked over to Jack, rubbed his face gently on Jack's torso, and rested his head there. A soft energy was in the air. As soon as Jack stopped trying to internally control him, Thor was able to connect with him. Jack was able to process his feelings, to make sense of and become conscious of a pattern that had been harming him in every aspect of his life. He was able to learn a new way of behaving that got him the attention he was craving. He no longer needed to portray himself as big and strong. Authenticity, the courage to speak his truth, and congruency were the answers.

Samantha. No Need to Try. Allow.

Then there was Karen. Karen was a small-business owner. She was in a new relationship, and her business was in its first year. We sat down in my broodmare stall, which had been converted into an office, to have a check-in before going out to greet the horses. Karen and I plopped down on the couches, and she began telling me how things were going. She often felt disconnected from herself. She was worried about giving herself over to this new relationship. She was worried about her business not growing quickly enough. She was worried about not making enough money. She was anxious that she wasn't putting her attention in the right direction. Karen was all over the place. She was dabbling in this and that and was in a frenzy most days, not really ever getting anything done. She wanted to feel calm, clear, and connected.

It was a beautiful summer day. The sun was shining, the grass was lush, and the horses were munching away. As we approached the gate to the paddock, I reminded Karen that we were moving into the horses' space, that this was their home, and that we needed to be respectful as we went in to greet them. Karen was going to connect with each horse and choose the one that she felt most drawn to or the one that seemed most drawn to her.

The horses continued grazing, looking more interested in eating than in engaging with Karen. Then all of a sudden, Samantha, a 6-year-old black-and-white paint mare, lifted her head, began walking towards Karen, and then stopped right beside her. Samantha was new to the horse work and came from a place where she was rarely handled. She was so disinterested in people that sometimes it was even difficult to halter her. I wondered whether or not she truly wanted to be a part of the healing work because of the way she usually ignored people. Today was different: She was clearly eager to work with Karen.

We brought Samantha in from the paddock and into the round pen, where I turned her loose. That gives the horse a chance to sniff (the horse's dominant sense) and get used to their surroundings before I invite the client into the round pen. Karen and I stood outside the round pen for a few minutes, watching Samantha roam around. Then I asked Karen to turn towards me as I turned to face Samantha. I asked her to close her eyes and invited her to do a body scan. Leading her through a scan of her entire body, from the top of her head to the tips of her toes, I asked Karen whether there was a particular area in her body that was standing out, calling for her attention. Karen said her chest. It felt really tight. I asked her if her chest could talk, what might it say. She said "release me." As Karen walked into the ring, she went directly over to Samantha. She started trying to connect with Samantha by petting her, whispering sweet nothings into her ear, trying to find her sweet spot, and telling her how beautiful she was. Then she closed her eyes and tried to connect with Samantha that way. Samantha's response was to walk away, pay little attention, and focus on what was going on outside. She walked to the other side of the pen. This experience went on for a few minutes. I could see the disconnect between them. Samantha was clearly not interested. I gently asked Karen what was going on.

"I am trying to connect," she said, "and it's not working."

I asked her, "What would connection look like if you stopped trying? What does connection look like without touching? What if you could just be?"

What transpired next was a beautiful miracle. Karen sat down in the round pen and just let herself be. She stopped trying. She stopped petting. She stopped whispering sweet nothings into Samantha's ear. She simply sat there. After a minute or so, Samantha walked over and nuzzled the top of Karen's head, then rested her head on Karen's shoulder. I could feel the connection in the air. Karen wasn't trying or forcing or working at it. Horse and human were just being themselves. Two species coexisting. A warmth filled my heart.

I then invited Karen to thank Samantha and asked her to exit the round pen. I asked her how the experience had felt.

Karen responded, "Wow, I didn't have to do anything. The less I tried, the more I just sat there and did nothing, and the more she wanted to be around me. What a lesson. I can connect without touching, without trying, without buttering up. The connection is there, I just have to be in it."

Karen called me a few weeks later and told me how she had been practicing this new principle in her life and that it had yielded many changes. She was using way less energy, she wasn't trying to impress her partner anymore, and she had way more love to give. It was in the trying, the forcing, that her connection was lost. It was by allowing herself to simply be that the connection was restored.

My personal story, along with many client stories, shows the power of horses to help people reconnect with themselves. In the traditional way of working with horses, the human dominates and puts their desires above those of the horse. In FEEL work, I have become aware of each horse's individual personality, strengths, deeper needs, and purpose. The horse remains connected to themselves and to their true nature. Astella, because she was pushed so hard as a show horse, is really helpful at helping people see their own patterns of pushing themselves too hard and helps them approach personal challenges with a more compassionate heart. Mandy, who has nurturing energy, helps people connect to the softness in their hearts. Lucky holds a beautiful space for people to work through their grief and sadness. Buck helps people learn to set boundaries and be assertive. And Duncan, the unexpected member and wild card in the herd, brings laughter and lightness into people's hearts.

In a culture that elevates the mind and intellect over intuition and the body's senses, horses are a powerful reminder to us: being present and congruent with our feelings is the first step to knowing thyself and being true. I was being rewarded by our culture for moving fast and thinking fast. Unfortunately, in my rush to appear successful on the outside, I suffered greatly on the inside. The FEEL work helped me to slow down and reconnect with myself, my surroundings, and what was important to me: self-acceptance, being present, and being congruent with my true nature.

Jennifer Schramm

Jennifer Schramm is a Registered Counsellor, Life Coach and certified Facilitated Equine Experiential Learning Practitioner who offers equine-assisted self-discovery as an approach to energy healing, skill-building, and personal development.

Working with horses has opened Jennifer's life in ways she never could have imagined, she knows how much others can benefit from this interspecies connection, and how profound and life-changing these experiences can be.

Her mission is simple: To help others stop living in their head, and start living in their heart.

Since horses are so attuned to non-verbal cues, Jennifer believes they act as human mirrors, providing transparent, immediate, and non-judgmental feedback on how we're relating to ourselves and our environment.

In guiding us to this place of self-awareness, horses can teach us how to rebuild trust in ourselves and others, communicate honestly, create healthy boundaries, develop confident leadership skills, and nurture our deepest passions. By giving people an opportunity to have their stories reflected back to them through the eyes of horses, Jennifer hopes to help others ride in new directions in their life, break free of their fears, and find the inner peace and self-acceptance they've been craving.

For more information please contact Jennifer at
www.unbridledexperiences.com
or email her at Jennifer@unbridledexperiences.com.

CHAPTER 3
Living My Soul's Calling
By Wendy Golding

I found my soul's calling through the wisdom, healing, and connection with horses. This is my story. I found out I really was a shining being who could live in joy and bring joy to everything around me. I discovered how to live, really live from my heart space, trusting my intuition, knowing who I am, loving that person, and trusting who I had become. I am a part of life—one soul that is one with the energy of the universe.

But first, I needed to become whole. It has been a long and rewarding journey in this lifetime, and the horses have been there all the way. With very few memories of my childhood, my earliest and fondest recollection of my father showed him down on his hands and knees cavorting around the living room like a horse and inviting me to jump on his back to go for a ride. I clambered aboard and yelled "giddy up" to get my horse to go faster.

I was abused as a young girl and this shaped all parts of my life. I was naturally shy and this experience caused me to create huge walls around my young, tender heart. I learned to survive by disassociating, it was easier for my mind to leave while the abuse was happening, yet I never knew consciously what this behavior was or what it meant until much later in life. I became very serious and people viewed me as somehow apart and aloof, my emotions were never expressed. My strong intuitive abilities somehow became locked inside my body.

There was no connection to my body; somehow I learned to survive through my mind. Combined with a learning disability that was never diagnosed, life in my early structured years became a struggle and recurring nightmares became part of my dreamtime. I became very small and my light was dim.

During this painful time in my childhood, the horses called to me. There was a driving need to be around them, but I didn't know how to manifest it. Another flashpoint of memory is visiting the home of one of my parent's friends who had a daughter a year older than me, At 10 years of age, she was horse crazy: every inch of her bedroom was covered with pictures, books, paintings, figurines, anything to do with horses. She loved to draw them and horses were what she talked about endlessly. I was so envious! Here was someone so passionate about horses and they came alive for her.

This realization led me to understand that I needed to express MY love of horses and had to step out of my shell and ask my parents to help me realize my dream of becoming closer to horses. During that time, the way to be around horses was to take riding lessons. As I recall, I badgered my parents unmercifully for what felt like a long time. They did not understand my fascination with horses. My parents were British and their knowledge of horses was as a farm animal. However they found an incredible stable in Niagara on the Lake, where you could not ride the horses until you learned to groom them and muck out their stalls. Being very impatient, it seemed forever before I got on the back of a horse. In retrospect, this was the best way of being introduced to horses; it was the start of being in relationship with these magnificent beings. Still being very shy, I didn't socialize very much with the other girls, but you could always find me in the confines of the horse stall or cleaning the leather of the bridles and saddles. My mother could never interest me in cleaning the house, but working with leather was a whole different story. My week revolved around the day I could be at the horse barn. I started to blossom and my confidence grew as I quickly gained the skills to start going over small jumps. Of course, as with any rider, I fell off a number of times. With developing back pain, my parents sent me to a back specialist in Toronto. This doctor devastated my world: The x-rays showed deformed vertebrae in my lower back with the consequence that I had to stop riding immediately and was told that I could never do any sports or any physical activity for the rest of my life. I was crushed and retreated even further inside myself. My confidence slowly seeped away.

Much later in life, I understood my back pain started at the age of 11 when I repressed all the anger and rage arising from the painful experience of a young girl being controlled against her will. I lived with ongoing and neverending back pain until I was 55 years old after healing the emotional trauma. There was no way to express my emotions in the very proper British household I was raised in so I became a quiet rebel. Anything my father asked me to do, I did the exact opposite. I fought against control and that became a lifelong pattern of needing to control everything around me.

Life became relatively uneventful and through my teenage years and as a young adult, I learned to wear a number of masks that hid what I was really feeling and thinking, even from myself. Being a highly sensitive person, I was overwhelmed with the energy of other people's emotions in large groups. All emotions carry an unseen energy that can be felt in the body; for instance, if you walk into a room and there is someone very angry, they don't need to say a word yet your mood is impacted as you respond to that energy. I did not understand why people liked going to parties. For me the energy was crushing. In combination with my introverted nature, it became a constant struggle to become a part of the social world.

Meeting my first husband when I was 13 years old, I was attracted to the big Ukrainian family ambiance where emotions ran rampant. I lived vicariously through this big family, getting married just out of my teens to escape a stilted and pretentious life with my parents. After suffering a very abusive marriage, I left my husband and became a single parent with two young children which cemented the walls that I built around myself as a young girl. In my 30s the dream of being with horses came alive again. A physiotherapist said the thinking around horseback riding and back issues had changed. Horseback riding can develop abdominal muscles that can support a poor back. I jumped at this. Living in Mississauga, I went to the closest horse barn I could find, only to be very disappointed. I came at my appointed lesson time and the horse was already saddled up and waiting for me and at the end of our lesson, the horse was handed off to someone else. The memories of that close relationship with a horse were not present.

Joining the Governor Generals Horse Guards, GGHG, which performed parades for visiting dignitaries, musical rides, and other exciting events, was a milestone for me. Dressed in a helmet with full military regalia, carrying a sword, it was so much fun galloping down the field with the rest of your Calvary unit yelling "charge!" I could feel myself coming back to life! We became partners with our horses as we traveled together on busy city streets and strange locations. Ralph, our leader, had amazing confidence in me and trusted me with his personal horse, Shilo—a magnificent steed who took me on many journeys. Shilo and I became one, whether it was winning ribbons at a Hunter Jumper show, doing an intricate musical ride, or sliding down a huge sand dune. Riding embodied absolute freedom. At first it was physical freedom, moving with this huge animal underneath me with the wind blowing my hair, I left all my problems behind. Then, over the years, being with the horse embodied emotional and spiritual freedom.

There was also a small polo club associated with the GGHG and my son suggested we take some lessons. What great fun! Coming from the very restrained, controlled military riding to galloping down a field chasing a ball was so releasing! I continued to voice my rebel call as I galloped down the field. I realize now the horses gave back to me my voice. Later, after moving to the Toronto Polo Club, they banned my conduct, calling it intimidating behavior. In the meantime Ralph again blessed me with Shilo as my polo partner. Monty, a 15-year-old small, but mighty black thoroughbred, came into our life for my son David to ride. It was a wonderful way as a single mom, to have fun and connect with my teenage son.

This started a decade of enjoying the sport of kings with many horse partners. When David chose to leave the sport of polo, Monty became my own polo pony. While Shilo and I had an incredible bond, Monty was my teacher in life, especially learning about developing a deeper relationship with these incredible beings. Monty's original name was WASP and it was very fitting for the mask he was wearing around people. People probably thought we deserved each other. We knew he had been abused with his previous owners, he couldn't stand still being tied in the aisle of the barn and you couldn't go near him holding a whip. He responded with stark terror. However, instead of being docile, he met life head-on with a very feisty manner. He let you know in no uncertain terms when he didn't like something. With his fiery spirit, I had trouble controlling him on the polo field; all he wanted to do was charge madly up and down the polo field. In addition, when you took him for a trail ride, he saw open fields and thought it was a great place to run. I was boarding Monty at the Club Manager's boarding stable and he could see firsthand the issues Monty and I were having. The manager said "I can solve this behavioral issue; I will run him up and down the arena until he tires and gives up." Well you can guess how that turned out: the manager gave up, Monty did not!

That summer there was a polo expert from the United States coming to host a clinic. Being one of the first ones to sign up, I thought this would be the answer to the problems I was having with Monty. The morning of the clinic the polo expert asked for a horse to demonstrate with. My hand shot up so fast and I thought great, he can fix Monty. Imagine my chagrin, when Monty was the perfect horse all day. I talked with the expert after the clinic and asked him how I could ride Monty in the same way. His answer to me was one I will never forget: "Monty is a very intelligent horse and he doesn't respect you. Until you earn his respect, you will not have a good relationship." So then I asked a really stupid question and said how long will it take? And his answer was, "it all depends on you." I was so frustrated. Here I was looking for answers and I just had more questions. However this was the turning point in my relationship with Monty and with all horses. I realized that they were sentient creatures: horses were intelligent, sensitive beings with emotions just like people. I changed the way I thought about horses, how I behaved with horses, and how I connected with horses. I am so glad Monty continued to be the rebel forcing me to listen to him.

Monty did not want to be restrained in any manner, very much like myself I realized. I found relationships with humans restricting. It was easy to give, but so hard to receive. Intimacy was not something I invited into my life; instead I needed to control everything around me. This was the only way I felt safe. I was in survival mode but certainly not thriving. With Monty I found myself being vulnerable and inviting him to join me in this dance of relationship. Over the next six months I changed ingrained patterns that had become so automatic over the years. I lowered the walls that I had built around myself as a form of protection. I gave up the notion of being constantly in control. I became authentic with Monty, sharing my doubts and fears, my hopes and dreams. We became partners. My heart opened to his heart. I became real for the first time in my life. Who I was on the inside matched who I was on the outside. Two beings so very wounded came together with hearts ready to risk once more. This was the beginning of a new way of being with horses—through heart connection.

However this was not only with horses. Coincidentally, or not, this is the same time that my heart opened to Andre after 18 long years of being a single parent. Andre and I had been business partners for seven years and had a very strong spiritual connection. I remember sitting in a restaurant where Andre would share his writings about the meaning of life. When Andre's marriage ended, it was like we had met for the first time and saw each other in a new light. Our relationship blossomed very quickly, an absolute knowing bringing the two of us together in a deep soul connection. Without Monty's help, I could not have stepped into a healthy relationship with an open heart. I was whole and balanced ready for a new life partner and for what Spirit had in store for my soul's calling.

Monty and I became a force to be reckoned with on the polo field. Monty, this little black horse, could run at the speed of light, turn on a dime, and feared nothing. At the time I was playing, most of the players were men and they thought nothing of this little horse with a woman rider. Polo is much like hockey, and one of the strategies is to have your horse bump the other horse off the line of the ball. Monty loved to bump other horses. His fierce spirit awakened mine which had become very compliant. Not only did I become more assertive in polo, I became more assertive in all areas of my life.

Unbeknownst to me, Monty was weaving the fabric and leading the direction my life was meant to go in. He had very firm ideas about what this should look like. Monty became a very powerful healer for all kinds of people. As we helped each other open to our emotions, he became a very affectionate horse and would lick your neck and face with his very big, thick tongue. I became a great hugger. We learned to trust together. My intuition, which had been locked away for so many years, bloomed and flourished.

At the age of 37 years, Monty chose to pass on to the other side still being in good physical and mental health. He rejoiced in the teachings and healings he helped create. In fact he was even participating in workshops up until the time of his transition. To this day, Monty remains my powerful spiritual guide as I continue to live my soul's calling.

In the year 2000, I fell off a horse, and herniated a disc in my neck. At this point, Andre and I had bought a small horse farm where we kept 12 horses. We had our own marketing business and any spare time was spent with the horses. We were living an idyllic life or so we thought. It was exhilarating, but there was no deep meaning to our lives. When the neurosurgeon said I could never play polo again and never ride a horse again, I was absolutely devastated for the second time in my life. Horses were my life; it was where I stood in my power and felt alive. However Spirit had something else in mind.

This was a major, life-changing experience for me and our horses. Looking back, I am in such gratitude for the way fate stepped in to open the gateway for my soul's journey. Wanting, needing something else I could be passionate about, I reconnected to my spirituality through shamanism. It is an ancient healing tradition and way of life with teachings focused on our connection to nature and all of creation. During a "rites of passage" ceremony, I was asked to focus on what I was going to do with the rest of my life. I received a vivid vision of helping people with horses while on the ground. I was transfixed. I had never done anything with horses on the ground throughout my entire time with them. This made absolutely no sense to me. However the strength of that vision touched a part of me so deep in my soul that I knew I had to pursue it. Through divine intervention I found EponaQuest and attended a workshop in Arizona. I saw horses, many different breeds and ages, that were something more than just a horse. They were wise teachers who helped people become whole again. Seeing the transformation in the participants, and feeling my own, I decided this is what I was going to do for the rest of my life. This was my life's calling!

I graduated as an EponaQuest Approved Instructor through the teachings of Linda Kohanov and Kathleen Ingram in 2006. The journey was not without trials and tribulations. My partner and I had built an international marketing company and after we found out I'd been accepted into the training program, three clients, one after another, declared bankruptcy. Financially, this was a major crisis for us. It looked like I would have to forgo the training. I was heartbroken; however my partner encouraged me to look beyond. After much soul-searching and connecting with our herd, we decided to trust the calling of the horses and proceeded with the plans for our future. Trusting this vision has led us both to a new way of life that is gratifying at a deep soul level. It initiated the start of many teachings and learnings deepening the horse human bond.

During my apprenticeship, I came to understand that my relationship to horses had expanded in ways that I had not imagined. With only a brief acquaintance, horses that I didn't know would respond to me and connect in a deep, profound way. During our practice sessions, my teachers observed my relationship with horses and started to give me horses that were reserved, aggressive, or just hard to work with. What I didn't understand at the time was that I was intuitively creating a heart connection with these horses before I ever asked them to do anything. From this place, the horses and I came together in partnership and we wanted to work together. My teachers would say "why are you approaching the horse, just do the activity." That was unthinkable to me. I wanted to connect with the horses at deep soul-to-soul heart connection. I had a rare opportunity to do this with Rasa during my training. It is a compelling, beautiful memory that stays with me. With melodic music playing in the background, Rasa and I moved in perfect harmony, first myself leading the dance, then Rasa, intertwined and together, our energies in perfect flow. I was transported to a higher consciousness, being in union with a being whose spirit was highly evolved.

With my partner Andre, Horse Spirit Connections was birthed in 2006, a not for profit corporation dedicated to bringing the teachings of the horses to people. Building on our initial training, we explored additional horse methodologies and created our own program. We called it FEEL (Facilitated Equine Experiential Learning). FEEL is a new way of being in relationship for horses and people. A heart-centered relationship with a horse creates a new, profound relationship with the people themselves. We created a place of discovery and reflection which touches the deepest part of our human spirit. This spirit is that part of our self which restores our wonder at the world and awakens our belief in magic, dreams, and possibilities.

We provided the space for safe and gentle interactions with horses, where people gain self-knowledge and acquire skills leading to positive life changes. Our vision is "Horses helping People and People helping Horses." We immediately saw the profound impact the horses had on people's lives, whether it was with adults, troubled youth, organizations, or corporations; transformation happened. Impact was made for thousands of people as they experienced the magic of connecting with our extraordinary horse teachers.

How do the horses create this magic?

What better way than to hear it directly from the horse's mouth. Thor, our master teacher, talks about how horses interact with humans in the book *Horse as Teacher*, Teaching the Wisdom of the Horse Ancestors chapter.[1]

"I spark the human's awareness by just being. A sense of calm prevails as I stand next to a person. My heart energy seeks to connect to the person's heart energy. I can see the person energized for a second, and then they relax and breathe in unison with my breath. Their mental busyness shifts lower into their chest, into their gut. I can feel settling as they connect their mind, body, and heart as one. When the human is in a place of openness, they can feel my message, interpreting my language by intuiting the information through their senses of hearing, seeing, and feeling. Feelings are the key. Emotions are crucial information for our survival. As horses we live by our instincts, we are very sensitive to our environment and all those who come in contact with us. We experience an emotion, take action, and go back to grazing. Emotions and experiences are just information that we process and let go. Emotions equate to energy in motion that ignites our cellular activation. We can read this activation in ourselves and other horses and humans, like reading a book of impulses they travel from the heart, to the brain, to the gut, and back. We horses have an enormous circuitry going through our intestines. Through this circuitry, we are very sensitive to currents of

energy that flow through us to the person we are connecting with. These electrical impulses can be fast or slow, spiking or calm. Our energy field is intertwined with the human energy field. There is a common harmonic evidenced by the strength and closeness of the horse human bond traveling through thousands of years... With humans, I sense their rate of breathing, beat of their heart, the muscle tension in their body, the smallest of their actions, their unique smell, and the cadence of their voice. Instinctively, I find that one piece of information the human needs to change in the moment to achieve a better balance between their body and their mind. Acting out my feelings, I reflect back to them the information they require."

Through Monty's guidance, a serendipitous accident, and a powerful vision, I discovered my soul's calling! I was living my dream with passion and joy, inspiring others to do the same. Now this shy, retiring person was standing up for what she believed in! The horses! I was their spokesperson and told their story with heart—through TV, radio, newspaper and magazine articles, whoever would listen to me. The horses brought me to a place in my life where I could connect to other people through an open-hearted connection filled with love and compassion. This is pure happiness!

Donna and Dusty

Through a long circuitous journey, Donna came to us as a last-ditch resort to find healing and peace. She had suffered incredible cruelty from ritual abuse starting from a young age. Prior to our meeting I had not been aware of the depths of depravity that exist in this world, and I had concerns about our abilities to help her. I connected with my mentor and the horse ancestors and asked if we could hold a safe container for her healing and they both said yes. An incredible courage brought Donna to us. Knowing of the incredible work of the horses and our spiritual coaching, she dipped her feet in the water and said she would try. This is a person who lived in constant fear, actual terror the likes of which I have never seen before. To deepen the experience for people, we often recommend a form of creative writing known as journaling. In this case, Donna panicked at the thought of writing anything down as she believed her tormentors would track her down and find her through her penned thoughts.

Donna's first session was with Dusty, one of our elder horses, a chestnut thoroughbred, who holds a quiet, yet strong space for people with an incredible heart energy. Donna walked into our old, weathered barn with faltering steps and was invited to go into the stall with Dusty, after first asking permission from Dusty. The intent was to do a heart connection with Dusty and spend reflective time with her. Donna stood in the doorway of the stall, unsure of what to do and started to talk to me. With encouragement I suggested that Dusty could better hear her story. She stepped into the stall with her energy very small, her body almost crouched over in fear. After hearing the description of a heart-connection technique, Donna placed her hand on Dusty's chest, over her heart area and placed her other hand over her own heart. Donna then breathed out through her heart, allowing her heart to open just a little bit. With that opening of heart energies, the healing energy from Dusty's heart flowed through her hand, up her arm into her own chest. Afterwards Donna talked about the warmth of the energy spreading throughout her whole chest.

During the experience Donna's body changed, her face softened, her eyes fluttered shut, her chest opened, and her shoulders went back. In a voice hesitant at first, she told Dusty about her shocking experiences and the humiliation and shame she felt at the things that she had been forced to do as a young child and then as an adolescent. While tentative at first, the words poured out bringing pent-up emotions to the surface. Then healing tears flowed gently down her cheeks and fell onto her chest. Throughout, Dusty held an incredible space for Donna to release her pain. As Donna's breath slowed, Dusty moved to place her nose on Donna's chest and then wrapped her head and neck around the back of Donna giving her a great big horse hug. There was a softening throughout Donna's body and this marked the beginning of Donna's healing with the horses. This journey sparked a deep abiding love affair with horses.

What a gift to be able to bring healing and joy to the many people we've been in contact with over the years. It became a time of learning to open my heart to people, being in a place of trust, letting the control go. In the beginning as I experienced the opening of my heart, I could feel a physical ache in my chest, like the muscles were actually stretching to accommodate the love and compassion. It was always easy to trust animals; people were so much more difficult. It was now a time of connecting heart-to-heart with people knowing we are all connected and all one.

Dusty's sage wisdom shines through her eyes

Wendy and Shilo as one after piercing the target with her sword!

Wendy celebrating life with Monty

Redman and Contendor together in harmony
before Redman's world was shattered

Thor's incredibly powerful presence embraces everything around him

But Spirit was not done yet!

Throughout the same period, my continuing love affair with shamanism opened many gateways to that something greater: a higher spiritual consciousness accessible for people, animals, and nature. Shamanism is not a course of study; it is a journey and a way of life. It is a way of looking at and relating to life from a broader perspective and engaging more fully with your everyday life. Up to this point, I had felt lonely and apart from everyone except for animals. Now I felt connected and at one with Spirit—I wasn't alone anymore. My heart opened wider.

Through this new expansive viewpoint, I learned that every species has a collective higher consciousness. Monty and our herd were delighted to teach me about the horse ancestors and the ascended horse beings from where a higher horse consciousness and ancient wisdom flows. Horses naturally step into this place of unification and align themselves with the profound and sage wisdom of their many descendants who came before. Imagine my delight when I learned how to connect with these mystical spiritual beings myself and access this current of knowledge from ancient times to beyond the present. The energy and the wisdom of the horse ancestors are very real to me and provide incredible support from holding sacred space to specific healing advice.

My spiritual relationship with the horses continues to evolve, leading me beyond the stars, leaping into higher consciousness with both humans and horses.

And it doesn't stop there! My soul's calling continues.

In 2008, Monty and our herd of horses conveyed the message that it was time for us to teach other people the magical healing power of the horses. The FEEL Certification training program was created with many talented and gifted instructors including Kathleen Ingram, one of my original teachers. Initially teaching out of our horse facility in Ontario, we brought the FEEL training program to British Columbia in 2014. What a gift of trust it was to work with one of our graduate's herd of horses. It confirms a universal raising of consciousness for all horses. Now aligned with Wilfrid Laurier University, we are teaching FEEL specifically for mental health professionals. The horses are so excited as we continue to touch more and more people who find their calling to do this compelling work with the horses.

"My time and experience in the FEEL Certification program has been life changing to say the least. I walked in my old self and am emerging a new wholly transforming person.... I have been able to literally witness myself evolving and changing more often than not moment by moment throughout this 6-month course. This program has enhanced my life on so many levels and has also helped to bring the JOY back into my life that has been missing for such a very long time... My experience in your program has fueled this joy that this work brings to me. This is why I

want to do this work to help to respark the JOY and help to reignite the fire of passion in others... That is why I became a Certified FEEL Practitioner! Your program is one of the most comprehensive, well laid-out programs I have participated in. It has filled in the gaps missing in other programs. The way in which you bring this work to your clients and trainees is with a tremendous amount of integrity, authenticity, and respect which deeply honors all who participate, both horses and humans. What you and Andre do is a great gift that I hope to watch you continue to share and also be a part of... Thank you, thank you, thank you for a most wonderful and life transforming experience and opportunity to take this amazing work with horses out to others."

Kamille Hottinger
Arlington, Washington, US

The horses created an opening for my love of teaching to come forth. Teaching and inspiring others is easy when it is something I am so passionate about, something I believe in so strongly, and it is an ongoing delight. Not only do people learn how to deepen their relationship with horses, they deepen their relationship with themselves. I open my heart so others can do the same and find their passion.

I found my family in the community that we have created with the FEEL Alumni. Like-minded, passionate people coming together with a common goal—deepening the horse human bond.

Back to the Horses!

My absolute delight is seeing a horse, who is just a horse, transform into a wise teacher and healer. It is hard to describe in words, but it is a feeling, a knowing when a horse teacher gazes into your eyes, sends energy into your heart, and does something so unusual in order to reflect back to you a life lesson. Each horse journeys to this place in a different way and manner. Having one of our horses in a workshop do something so incredibly profound for someone, brings tears to my eyes, tears of such gratitude that these horses are so willing to be of service to us as humans with their huge hearts. Humans who throughout history have broken their spirit, caged them up trying to control them, and hunted them for food.

With our vision being "Horses helping People and People helping Horses" it was time to help the horses. Hearing the plight of more and more horses being abandoned, found starving, going to the meat market, broke my heart. We decided that whenever there was an opening in our barn we would rescue and rehabilitate a horse, helping the horse come back into a place of balance mentally, physically, emotionally, and spiritually. When we met some of the horses, they were just a shell, there was no spark left in their eyes, they were defeated. Bringing them back home to our sacred land, we let them become a horse again in a herd of nurturing sentient horses. Sometimes it took a month, sometimes it took two years. We listen to each horse to see what they need to heal. Once they are healed each horse is given the choice of whether they want to become a therapy horse or not. Most times they leap at the opportunity, if not we find them the home they want. As the horses walk along this path of being of service to people, they continue to heal past traumas and develop astonishing gifts. To me there is nothing more rewarding than seeing a horse come back to life, full of pride, thriving in the knowledge they have a purpose and can make a difference.

Every day I am inspired by the powerful teachings and healings of our magical horses and the courage of people who are choosing to create a life aligned from their heart. This is a story of an intimate and profound experience one of our clients had with Redman, one of our horse teachers.

Redman: The Wounded Healer

Redman evolved into an incredibly gifted empath and healer through an illness last fall. Sometimes the very experiences that wound us the most are also those from which we draw our greatest strength through a deep healing process. Redman is a Spotted Mountain Horse who originally came to us as my riding horse. He is incredibly sensitive to the emotions of his herd and the humans around him. In order to protect himself he had developed a mask of being a clown, lover boy, and overall foolish teenager. He engaged with people by pushing himself into their space with affection and constantly tested their boundaries. What we didn't realize—it was the intimacy he so wanted for himself but within a safe container.

Last fall Redman's herd consisted of Contendor, Paris, and Aria. Redman was the only male horse Contendor has ever allowed near his mares. Contendor is a wild stallion in spirit and very protective. Last summer Aria chose to become pregnant (Contendor believes he is the father!) and suddenly the herd dynamics totally changed overnight! From being Contendor's best buddy and playmate, Redman was shunned from the herd by both Contendor and Aria. He was literally driven away from them time after time. Suddenly Redman succumbed to a very strange illness. He was running a fever of 104.5 (very high for a horse), his legs swelled up, and his autoimmune system rebelled. Our vets, after numerous tests and consults with experts, were stumped! They came twice a day and kept changing medicines, hoping something would work.

We asked in ceremony what was wrong with Redman and we "heard" he was dying of a broken heart. He had been abandoned as a young horse and now this latest abandonment from his herd had triggered a strong PTSD reaction in his body. Friends of Redman around the world offered prayers for his healing. During one of our group workshops, all of us (horses and humans) performed many powerful and profound ceremonies for his recovery. We knew that unless we could heal him emotionally and spiritually, he would never recover his physical well-being. Our vet still doesn't understand what caused or cured his illness. He says very strange things happen here at Horse Spirit Connections!

When Redman recovered, we introduced him into Thor's herd where there were two other male horses, Thor and Spirit Walker. Redman had to start all over again and carve out his place in the herd dynamics. His demeanor changed and he owned his wisdom. It has been wonderful to see him step in the teacher role with Spirit Walker which has now evolved into the two of them playing together. What has been most intriguing has been the shift in his role of teacher and healer with humans. With a newfound maturity, he is accessing wisdom gained from his own wounding and the Horse Ancestors to allow him to have a basis for understanding and meeting both the pain and the potential for healing in people.

Redman and Laura

Laura had arrived at the farm on a cold and cloudy day. We had received a light dusting of snow the night before and everything looked so pristine. We decided to do a reflective session in the arena where we would be protected from the cold. As the horses were out in the paddocks, Laura and I went out into the fields to meet the horses and determine which horse was her teacher that day. The sun came out amid a backdrop of a brilliant blue sky when we began our walk into the fields where Redman's herd of eight horses lived. Forgetting a halter, I went back to the barn and it just so happened I picked up Redman's. Laura had already walked into the field and Redman very deliberately approached her while the other horses kept their distance. Normally this would be a very clear indication that Redman was to be her teacher that day. However, when I haltered him, he wouldn't budge. He was fully engaged but wouldn't come with us. I asked Laura to do a heart connection with Redman and while he moved his head closer to her body, he still would not come with us. Both Laura and I realized at the same time, he was telling us he wanted to work with Laura in the field with his herd.

After taking the halter off, Laura stood still with Redman and in the quiet connection, realized she had a hard time initiating and feeling a heart connection with another being whether horse or human. Further reflection led Laura to understand she had a resistance to claiming her power. By keeping her heart shut she limited her own power and didn't own it or take responsibility for it.

As she was speaking the words, Redman immediately dropped to his knees right beside her with no warning. Our horses use rolling or lying down in a teaching situation to speak about the strength in vulnerability—this is the most vulnerable position for a horse physically—however they usually move a little bit away and paw the ground before they lie down. The rest of the herd held a very sacred place standing in an arc around them at least 40 feet away. Dusty was the closest horse and she was licking and chewing for most of the time signifying she was actively engaged. Laura and I discussed spending time with the different horses to see how the heart connections might feel different with each one.

While we were talking, Redman lied down with his head resting on the snow and was making very funny movements with his lips in the snow. I invited Laura to kneel beside Redman and feel this precious gift he was giving her. After 15 minutes of deep stillness, she suggested going to visit the other horses and receive more teachings. As she started to leave, Laura realized it didn't feel right to leave this intimate connection with Redman and that this was a pattern of leaving and not claiming her power. She learned it was important to pay attention and listen to her heart; not to get "overruled" by her head (or by what she THOUGHT was going to happen).

Laura knelt down again and Redman whispered to her, a soft nicker but so different from any I have heard before and then lied flat out on the ground with neck and head on the ground and his legs totally stretched out. Afterwards Laura shared that it was so intimate: like being in bed with your lover.

After Redman stood up, he did a lot of expressive yawning (releasing) and then amazingly started to push Laura's boundaries. She learned how to set firm boundaries with her heart remaining open. At first this seemed so out of place, yet Redman wanted Laura to learn that when in intimate relationships, boundaries are healthy.

At this point Laura felt complete and we started to walk out of the field. As we were walking, Laura trusted her intuition and asked me if she could continue to stand in the field as she still felt the connection with Redman. For another 10 minutes Redman stood still, facing her squarely, head on and connected with Laura from 20 feet away. Then he lay down again and did it in a kind of semi-circle curve, so that his back end was pointed at her AND he could continue to see her (which he did the whole time). Laura took this as a validation of her experience—just in case she decided to doubt what had happened!

When Laura came out of the field she shared that the biggest message from Redman was she had the courage to claim her power just as he had that day with his herd! His new herd embraced his leadership in that moment, and fully supported and honoured him. By doing so they recognized him in his new identity of wounded healer— full of wisdom and grace. His willingness to be of service, through open heartedness and vulnerability, revealed his true strength and power.

From Laura: *There are so many lessons for me in Redman's story and in our experience together. In my own way, I've lived Redman's story of rejection from his tribe; I've experienced that feeling of not belonging anymore. So his courage to claim his gifts of healing and teaching in front of his new herd (especially in front of Thor the master teacher) inspired me in a profound way. But I think the most important message for me to remember is that the path to freedom and power, and the path forward, is through an open heart. I believe Redman and I were both initiated that day into a new way of being in the world. I am forever grateful to Redman, his herd, and you Wendy for this incredible learning and experience.*

Each day, each client reminds me of my soul's calling: being in partnership with horses! I celebrate how I am becoming more and more horse like! Living in the moment, heart centered, in harmony and balance, trusting my intuition, seeing the ripples flowing out and following them.

I also know my journey has just begun! And as you are reading these words, you are joining me on this magical journey with horses who can heal and transform. Magic can be part of your everyday world, too! Join with the herd and ask the horses to come into your dream space for healing. Start connecting energetically with the spirit of horses. Look at the pictures of our master horse teachers on our website.

By gazing into Contendor's eye—found on the home page of our Personal Discovery section of our website www.HorseSpiritConnections.com— let your soul be touched by his. Next, look for long distance healing with the horses as they expand their repertoire.

I invite you to find YOUR passion and most importantly LIVE IT. It will feed you in ways you can never dream of. Ask the horses to help you. YOU are a shining being!

"Life isn't about finding yourself life is about creating yourself"
—George Bernard Shaw

Wendy Golding

Wendy Golding is a trusted and respected leader in the field of Equine Facilitated Learning, a speaker, author, and President of Horse Spirit Connections Inc., a not for profit corporation dedicated to promoting transformation and personal growth through the wisdom of the horse.

Being passionate about horses all her life, Wendy took up riding again in her thirties and joined the Governor General's Horse Guards in Toronto, where she participated in the precision riding of military parades and the grace of musical rides. She loved the thrill of galloping down a field, sword at the ready, piercing a target, and raising it high in triumph! Wendy went on to play the noble sport of polo, experiencing that incredible trust that exists between horse and rider, in mutual partnership.

After a bad fall and serious injury to her neck, Wendy sought another way to express her passion for life and stay connected to horses. Shamanism was part of the answer. Wendy became a Shamanic Coach and Practitioner, learning the interconnectedness of all things and a way of seeing from the heart for the purpose of accessing spiritual guidance.

Combining this healing modality with the wisdom of the horse opened a new world. Wendy was thrilled to discover the EponaQuest Approach and become an EponaQuest Instructor. This was the magic she wanted to provide the world.

Wendy is a seasoned professional and entrepreneur with more than 30 years' experience in the corporate world. Her proven track record of successes include spearheading inaugural international projects while sitting on the Chamber of Commerce Board, Director of the Governor General Horse Guards, President of the Jaycees and co-owner of Winks & Ink, a multimillion dollar marketing and merchandising company.

Andre and Wendy went on to found Horse Spirit Connections located outside Toronto, Canada and created FEEL (Facilitated Equine Experiential Learning) services and programs for people of all ages. They provide a six-month intensive FEEL Practitioner Certification training program for practical training and experience in developing FEEL programs where the horse is valued for their role as a therapist and teacher.

Wendy invites you to awaken your spirit and to learn more about this special connection with horses at:
www.HorseSpiritConnections.com.
Email her at wendy@HorseSpiritConnections.com

CHAPTER 4

What Brings Me Joy

By Susan Collard

I never thought I would find myself here, in this place. A place where feeling joy is a regular occurrence. A place where I have a voice and know I am being heard. A place where I can live with an open heart, knowing it is safe to do so. A place where I live with the knowledge that Spirit resides within me and therefore is never far away. I find myself in this place of understanding where to help others in a profound way means I have to stay committed to my own healing journey and do the work.

Growing up in an alcoholic home meant life was very chaotic. From the perspective of a child, the unpredictable behavior I witnessed by those around me meant I didn't have control over my environment. Lack of control went along with not feeling safe.

Needs of the children often lagged behind those of the adults. Healthy boundaries simply didn't exist. I always felt like the odd person out in my family because I was the lone introvert. The other members of my family were extraverts who loved to party. I always wanted to belong, but never really did.

A traumatic experience at the age of 9 reinforced the belief that I was alone and unlovable. Since the adults in my life had not protected me and kept me out of harm's way, it must of been because I was not good enough to warrant that love and protection. That was how I viewed the world at the tender age of 9.

Several years later, I started taking horseback riding lessons. I realize now that the development of my close relationship with horses was analogous to a rescue. I can honestly say they rescued me, at the age of 11, and as a result I became entranced by these magnificent creatures. I was grateful to be able to escape to the barn. It was a way to forget everything else that was going on in my life. The stable became my refuge. This was the one place where I could simply be myself. It was also the place where I felt unconditional love. The horses would greet me when I came into the barn or approached them in the field. They were always present, they were accepting, and did not judge. I felt a real sense of freedom when I was with them. I attribute their presence in my life as having kept me from the temptation of drugs and alcohol as a young person. Not sure how my life would have turned out if the universe had not brought them to me.

Some years later, after a failed marriage and many attempts to "fix myself" through self-help books and seminars, I connected with a therapist who was very adept at helping trauma survivors. At one particular meeting, she posed the question "find something you love, something that brings you joy and make time to engage in that activity once a week." Coming up with a response was easy. It would have to involve horses in some way.

When I told my therapist that I loved horses and that being around them brought me immense joy, she smiled. She then proceeded to tell me about an experience she had had with a horse nine months earlier. She explained she had a fear of horses, stemming from a negative encounter with a horse many years before. She had been introduced to a FEEL (Facilitated Equine Experiential Learning) Practitioner who had offered to do a session with her to show her a new way of being with these amazing four-legged creatures. She was told no riding experience was necessary as she would be working with the horse on the ground.

As she described what happened during the session, tears began to flow down her cheeks. The impact of this event had the power to bring emotions to the surface, even nine months after it had taken place. I was very intrigued and told her I wanted to learn more. I wanted to learn about this new way of partnering with horses. She passed along the contact information of the FEEL Practitioner she had met with so I could hear firsthand what this work was all about.

I was unable to reach the FEEL Practitioner initially so I began searching for any program that would allow me to work with horses while helping others. Unconsciously I was probably hoping the horses would somehow be able to fix me. The next few weeks were filled with phone calls and research as well as reading everything I could get my hands on regarding the concept of horses as healers.

As I was reading these books, I began to think about horses in a different way. I became aware of all the ways horses were teaching us, instead of the other way around. One recurring theme which emerged that struck a chord with me was the richness of the relationship people were now having with horses. Relationships were evolving and humans were gaining a true understanding of how these sentient creatures thrived on the planet. Horses exhibited a natural curiosity, playfulness, great wisdom, mindfulness, acceptance, emotional agility, forgiveness, non-judgmental attitude, and a strong connection to other members of the herd as well as the horse ancestors. As I pondered this way of being that the horses modeled, I realized I too wanted to live this way. I wanted to live mindfully, be present to all things around me, accepting of others just as they are. I wanted to have meaningful connections with others, which meant living from a strong heartfelt place, just like the horses.

I continued my research on FEEL certification programs in Canada and came in contact with Wendy Golding at Horse Spirit Connections. Wendy allowed me to meet her herd and during the course of our initial conversation, it became clear this program was for me. This program would be a perfect way to marry my love of horses, my desire to help others, and maybe even incorporate knowledge I had gained from my university psychology degree. I applied to the six-month intensive training program and when I got the news I had been accepted, I was ecstatic. I immediately began fantasizing about having my own farm with my own herd of horses. I dreamt about having a steady stream of clients coming through the front gate, all of whom would have transformative experiences with the horses. I figured if this program could help with my healing journey, there were bound to be others like me out there in the world.

Over the next few months, as part of our FEEL training, we would learn about horse behavior, how to remain present—in our bodies, not our heads (a natural state for horses), how to expand and contract our energy fields, how to practice effective facilitation skills, understand the difference between authentic and false self, learn about the message behind the emotion, learn about spiritual oneness, and much more. I was eager to embrace these new skills. What I was not prepared for was how much I was going to learn about myself in the process.

As part of the training, experts were brought in to teach various aspects of the program. I felt honoured to meet these conscious and extremely wise women who had found a way to combine their existing skills in helping clients with the experiential component of partnering with horses. They were also very connected to the natural world and had strong spiritual beliefs, which resonated with me.

During the training, it was explained to us that in addition to learning this new material, we would have to conduct a full-day workshop with real live participants. We would be separated into two groups and would conduct the workshop at the end of our six-month program. This was no practice workshop, it was the real thing. We were also told that prior to the workshop we would have to facilitate a number of private sessions with practice clients. Fear was starting to creep in.

I asked several friends and colleagues if they would be interested in helping me by committing to three FEEL sessions within a specific time period. There would be no cost involved and all they needed to bring to each session was a notebook and an open mind. I soon had four willing participants. Due to the fact that I did not have horses of my own, I was going to have to rely on the generosity of a friend who was allowing me to work with her two horses as well as partnering with the herd at Horse Spirit Connections, where I was taking the FEEL program.

Practice Clients

I arranged my first few sessions with clients and they went along quite well at the beginning. Clients seemed happy to have developed new insights into themselves. Sometimes it was a totally new awareness of how their behavior impacted another being. Other times, it was a deeper understanding of the blocks that were holding them back from achieving a specific goal.

As I progressed however, I found it increasingly difficult to remain neutral and not get caught up with what the client was feeling during the session. I had difficulty staying grounded and felt I was up in my head most of the time, instead of in my heart. I was unable to settle into this new role and was being triggered by some of the experiences the clients were having with the horses. I was not able to simply be aware of the triggering situation, let it go, or promise myself to come back to it once the session was over. I was unable to move past it and return to a state of neutrality. At the end of each session, I was emotionally exhausted. I was trying to keep it all together but deep down, I knew I was not providing the best experience for the client.

During our FEEL training we had been taught how to create a bubble or a shell around ourselves to reduce the risk of negative energy belonging to others from impacting our body and aura. I wasn't having much luck with the bubble!

Another realization I had regarding my work with practice clients was around expectations. Expectations I had about my role as a facilitator and expectations of what the client's experience should look like. My perfectionist tendencies came bubbling up, which meant there was no room for error on my part. As for the client, I was convinced that each one would "see the light" and come to realize what gifted teachers the horses were. I wanted them, no I "needed" them to have an earth-shattering experience. Looking back on those moments, I'm sure it was the need to obtain approval from others that drove this desire. This desire likely originated from my younger self who longed for her parents' approval, that seldom materialized.

The insecurity I was feeling as a result of lack of experience with facilitating these FEEL sessions meant it was important to maintain some sense of control. I wanted to know at least at a high level what was going to take place during a session. I had all this training behind me, I had a fantastic mentor who was always accessible and would give me sage advice, I had very experienced horses to work with, and yet I was still unwilling to give up control. Once again the "trust" element came up. I did not trust myself or my higher power enough to let go. Mistrust towards others, a remnant of my adolescent years was now showing up in my role as FEEL Practitioner.

I knew horses would always take the lead because they knew what the client needed in that moment. I could at least trust that. But I was rigid in my thinking and felt it was necessary to have a plan. I needed to plan out what exercises would be best for the client in the first session, then the second, etc. If the plan was executed properly, things would go smoothly. This approach might have worked well in a business environment but I soon realized that to be successful with the FEEL work, things had to be different. It was also apparent that my refusal to let go, coupled with the strong desire to remain in control was having a negative impact on my personal relationships as well.

I knew that if I was serious about fulfilling the dream of having the horse farm and partnering with horses to help others, I was going to need some help. I decided to reach out to one of the FEEL trainers who was also a psychotherapist and asked if she would work with me. Thankfully she agreed and so began our partnership. We started meeting regularly, accessing the wisdom of the horses and the wisdom within myself.

Susan with Leo, a beloved FEEL Horse

Susan's herd of healing horses

Trusting My Intuition

One beautiful spring day, I arranged to meet a friend, who was also studying to be a FEEL Practitioner, at her friend's farm to work with the horses. We decided we would practice our newly honed facilitation skills with each other and then just hang out with the horses. We went out into the field to meet them. It was decided I would go first. After making a connection with Blackjack, a large black thoroughbred cross, I led him into the round pen. I was then guided through a body scan, one of the many exercises we had been taught to keep us grounded and in our bodies. Only then could I get clarity on my heart's desire. I stated that I wanted help from Blackjack with learning to trust my instincts. Into the round pen I went.

I walked to the center of the pen, made sure I was feeling centered, and proceeded to make a heart connection with the horse. I reminded him of my intention (heart's desire) and within minutes he came to me, nuzzled my right hand, travelled up my right arm to my face and then back down to my hand. Afterwards he turned and walked away, pivoting his front end around and positioning himself so that his back end was facing me. He slowly backed up and did not stop until his hind end was touching my arm and shoulder. He then leaned his weight into me. I froze, realizing I was in a very vulnerable position but not wanting to move away. I felt a strong physical sensation in my stomach and chest.

My brain was registering fear but my body was telling me something else. At that moment I had to decide–if I should respond to my brain and move away or listen to my gut and stay put. I decided to listen to my gut and trust my instincts. I knew I was safe right here, standing in this spot. There was no need to retreat.

Blackjack then shifted his weight from his right side to his left, quite relaxed, resting his back foot on the ground. After a few minutes I stepped away and moved back to the center of the pen. Blackjack followed and came right up to me, placing his muzzle against my stomach, as if to say "don't forget to trust your gut."

Upon reflection after the Reflective Round Pen exercise was over, my friend and I both agreed that this wise horse had known just what I needed to have a true experience of listening to my intuition, allowing it to guide me and keep me safe. Blackjack pushed me to the edge, wanting to see if I had the courage to remain still, as he leaned into me. My instincts told me I was safe and could remain there. Trusting my instincts was not a skill I had developed growing up. I had convinced myself that my intuition had not kept me safe as a child, so it was not to be trusted. This faulty thinking kept me stuck and deprived me of the experience of learning how to make sound decisions based on information from my sixth sense.

Like the scary experience in the round pen with Blackjack, as a youngster whenever I found myself in a fearful situation, I would actually leave my body. I had the sensation of floating up to the ceiling of the room or up in the sky and would peer down at myself, feeling very much like a separate entity or being in that moment. This response became so automatic during stressful situations that I would leave or dissociate without realizing I was doing it. Working with the horses has helped tremendously because they will only respond to me when I am totally present. The horses' immediate feedback reinforces the state of being that is crucial to remaining in my body. Horses are the perfect role models for staying in one's body, as they have evolved that way as a species in order to survive.

As I later reflected on what I'd learned from Blackjack that day, I thought about how I sometimes override the physical feelings I get when confronted with making a decision. I would stay in my head and try to figure it out, weighing the benefits and risks. Finally I would come up with what I thought was a logical decision. Yet what I have learned in recent years is that there are several areas of the body that provide invaluable information that can be processed and used, much the same way as our brain works. The information coming from our gut as well as our heart can be just as powerful as the neurons firing in our brain. My life would have evolved very differently if I had listened to that feeling in my gut, instead of ignoring it. The same could be said for taking down the wall which had been built around my heart, allowing me to hear its desires.

Boundaries

When I first started in the FEEL program, we were guided as to how to respect the boundary of a horse as well as how to let the horse know what our boundaries were. We learned about energy layers. This was all new to me and while I was fascinated by the concept of these layers, I knew I would be challenged with respecting boundaries with horses. Asking permission to move closer to a horse or to touch a horse was very foreign to me. My training from the time I was a teen, was to control my equine partner. I was to dictate to them what needed to be done and when. Decisions were primarily the rider's responsibility, not the horse's. One of the things I longed for whenever I went up to the barn as a young person was to be able to hug and touch the horses at liberty and as much as I wanted. Not sure if it was a strong need for connection, unconditional love, or simple touch that drove my need to behave in this manner.

The real learning experience for me with setting and respecting boundaries came with one of the horses at Horse Spirit Connections. Her name was Papi. Papi was the lead mare of one of the herds at the farm and was a very gifted teacher. My experience with Papi in the round pen was very powerful. I was moving from the center of the round pen and approaching Papi with my arms out to the side, palms facing forward, in order to feel the different energy layers. I felt a tingling sensation and heat on my hands as I passed through all three layers. When I got to the final layer which was about 2.5 feet from her shoulder, I stopped. I then turned and faced the same direction she was facing and slowly inched my way closer to her shoulder. I so desperately wanted to reach out and stroke her neck but I knew it wasn't allowed. It was taking all my willpower to restrain myself. So I figured if I kept my hands by my side, I could wiggle closer to her shoulder and see if maybe, just maybe, she would allow me to touch her body. I made it all the way to within 2 inches from her side. This is when she turned her head around and gave me the look that said, "that's as close as you'll get." She was very clear about her boundaries.

Another horse who was a wonderful teacher for me with respect to boundaries was a spotted Mountain horse called Redman. Whenever I was in the field with the horses at liberty, Redman would enter my personal space without a care, shove me with his head, and then nibble at my coat or gloves. He is such an amazing big-hearted horse that it was always challenging for me to set a boundary and stick to it. Admittedly while I did enjoy the attention, after witnessing the same behavior many times, I knew Redman was simply pushing me to set a boundary with him. I was able to finally set that boundary and experience what it was like to have my boundaries respected. It was very empowering. It was also incredible to witness how the heart connection between us was maintained even after a boundary had been set.

I think a part of me always feared that if you set a boundary with another being, they would feel rejected somehow. I feared they would leave and not return. Growing up, I was never shown how to set boundaries with others, whether they were the physical or emotional variety. Boundaries were a foreign concept. In the absence of boundaries, others were free to walk all over me, taking what they wanted, when they wanted it.

Energy Modulation

Another learning opportunity arose with a lesson on how to increase and decrease my energy levels. By developing this skill, I knew I could achieve a heightened and empowered sense of presence while watching my energy and the horse's energy interact. The Active Round Pen exercise involves standing in the center of a pen, roughly half the size of an average arena and directing the horse to move at a certain speed and direction by using voice commands or by simply pushing energy out or contracting it in. It was instrumental in getting me out of my head and into my body. It also showed me very quickly when I was not being consistent, not being assertive enough, or unclear about my intention.

The frustration I experienced with a mare named Paris, who is a master teacher when it comes to this exercise, was another great moment. I had learned that when frustration arises, to think about what action is being taken that is not effective and then change it. In the past, I would likely continue to feel frustrated and gradually become angry when something wasn't working. Knowing what questions to ask makes it so much easier now to return to a state of balance.

I have been able to see over time, while practicing this skill, how much more effective I can be as a leader in the work I do. I am more cognizant of the importance of clarity, the power of intention, and understand much better how breath affects my energy level. In my personal life, being open and honest about my intentions when engaging with others or making an important decision is crucial. Firstly though I need to have clarity around what I truly want, only then can I state my intention to another individual.

Feeling Joyful

One cold winter's day, as I drove up to the farm to meet with my therapist for one of our FEEL sessions, I was thinking about whether there was a particular issue I might want to work on. In the past, I would stress about not knowing in advance what my intention or agenda was for our time together. But on that particular day, I was feeling good about the awareness I had regarding the benefits of letting go. The work with the horses was helping me to trust that what I needed on that day would materialize. When I arrived at the farm, we met in the meeting room which was cozy and warm, on account of the wood stove ablaze in the corner. We chatted for awhile and then as we had done many times before, walked up to the barn to connect with the horses. As I entered the barn, I felt an immediate sense of release. I had been unaware of how much stress and tension I was holding in my body until that moment. By their mere presence, I was feeling more at peace. I stood by the stall door, breathed deeply and shortly thereafter got the message from one of the horses to "let go, it is safe to do so."

After connecting with a beautiful grey mare named Rosa, I proceeded to take her into the arena. My therapist guided me through a body scan and as a result, I was able to feel energy swirling around in my chest. After breathing into that part of my body, I got the message that my intention for the session was to experience joy and exhilaration. When I turned around to face Rosa, I made a heart connection and told her what my desire was.She immediately started prancing around the perimeter of the pen, calling out to her herd mates. I was encouraged to let go and do whatever felt right in the moment.

I stepped into the pen, walked over to the rail, took a deep breath, and started skipping around the inside of the pen. The feeling of freedom and playfulness was exhilarating. I even broke into song. As I moved around the pen, I was aware of Rosa maintaining her presence beside me, trotting along, deliberating lifting her feet high. It was great fun! Whenever I stopped moving, Rosa did as well. As I changed direction, she followed. After a few minutes, I stopped skipping and moved to the center of the round pen. I stretched my arms out wide, threw my head back and began to spin around. Rosa stood and watched. After a few rotations, I began to feel lightheaded so I grounded myself and stood still. Rosa immediately started cantering around the pen, hugging the rail. I could feel her exhilaration and joy as she moved her well-toned body. After completing several turns around the pen, I looked at Rosa, slowed my breathing down, and bent over at the waist, signaling for her to slow down. She stopped, walked into the center to join me and brought her head up to meet mine. It was magical! The entire time I was in the round pen with Rosa, it felt like we were in sync with one another, feeding off each other's energy.

After placing Rosa's halter on her, I led her back to the barn, all the while feeling as though my heart was going to burst open, it was so full of love. Feelings of pure joy and unconditional love were rare experiences in my life. This was part of the reason I so desperately wanted to just stand in the barn next to her and allow the feeling to continue to wash over me. I didn't want the feeling to dissipate.

Oneness of Spirit

There were times over the course of the six-month program, that I felt somewhat separate from the other women. Many of them seemed to be able to connect to the horses and the horse ancestors telepathically, without much effort or so it seemed. I struggled with this. As we had gotten to know one another during those months, I came to admire the spiritual connection some of them had with animals, with nature, with all beings. I thought about my own life and how I had been searching for a way to foster those connections. I also wanted to find a way to connect with my higher power. I was having a hard time and was feeling a little stuck. I was sure of one thing, I felt closer to my higher power when I was out in the woods or by the water, not when I was sitting in a place of worship made of bricks and mortar.

As I reflect now on the religious teachings from grade school and church services, as a young person, I remember the notion of God/Spirit as this all powerful being that was completely separate from me. As I had seen others do, my prayers and questions about my life's purpose were always being directed out there....out into the ether. My prayers never seemed to be answered though so I stopped communicating all together. The religious doctrines and the fear-based mentality that church elders were preaching just didn't make sense to me. I felt there had to be something else out there, but I wasn't sure what. I wondered if I would recognize it if I stumbled upon it.

My FEEL journey thus far had taken me from a place of feeling alone and very disconnected to Spirit to a place of opening my heart, with a desire to reach out. I could not envision what this relationship with Spirit would look like but I knew that I wanted one. In the meantime, I was being guided by some very wise women to "be present and listen." On those rare occasions when I did tune into messages from the horses, I kept hearing "stop running and just be still." I figured this was a good place to start.

Then one day I entered the pen with Rosa, the beautiful grey mare who I had come to know as a very special "Wounded Healer." I went into the centre as I had been instructed to do. I stood and faced Rosa and made a heart connection with her. The connection manifested as a warm feeling in my chest with the physical sensation of energy swirling around in a circular pattern. She turned to face me and was only about 8 feet away. As she walked directly to me, I was transfixed by her gaze. There was a soft, gentle look in her eyes. She seemed to be staring directly into my soul. It was as though my higher power was contained within her beautiful body. With our hearts connected, I felt as though we were a single entity. It was as if our bodies had merged together. I felt close to her, spiritually, emotionally, mentally, and physically. There was a peacefulness and calmness that came over me, something I had never experienced before. It is difficult to find the words to express what transpired. The closest I can come in the way of a description is that it was a "state-of-grace" moment.

All the trainers and program participants in the arena who were watching Rosa and I interact, no longer seemed to be there. They simply faded away. In that moment of pure connection, pure love, it was only Rosa and me.

The memory of that event, which took place over two years ago, is so ingrained in my body that if I close my eyes, I imagine myself there, standing in the horse arena. It is as if the memory has been forever stored in the cells of my heart. So when I have moments of doubt that my higher power is present, I simply close my eyes and remember that day in the round pen with Rosa.

Telling a story of one's own experience is always risky business. There is always the chance that when the story being told relates to an arduous struggle in search of answers, the pain of allowing one's vulnerability to be seen can be too much to bear. It can stop the creative process and move the writer to want to change it to a more benign story. I can honestly say working with horses as well as many other wise teachers, has brought me to this place. The place of being able to recognize the healing energy that is present when one's heart is open and vulnerable. After all, the message behind the emotion of vulnerability is that something significant is about to change or be revealed. What has been revealed to me is the realization that what I've been searching for all these years resides within me.

From within, I have found the willingness to reach out and ask for help, trust my intuition, trust others, understand my emotions, and set boundaries. I now get the importance of clarity and stating my intention. I get the importance and power of the human breath. I have the knowing that Spirit will always be there for me because he resides within me. These are all things the horses have taught me. The knowledge gained from their own life lessons as well as wisdom from the horse ancestors have contributed to my healing journey. I have come to understand how precious the gifts are they generously share with us humans. Because of them, I have also come to understand the gifts I bring to the world.

My plans for the future involve a partnership with a dear friend who is also a FEEL Practitioner. She has recently purchased Meadowlark Farms, located near Hamilton, Ontario and we will be establishing our FEEL practice there. We are currently looking for rescue horses to bring back to the farm. Our goal is to offer them freedom of choice within a natural setting where no demands to be ridden will be made. All we ask of the horses is a desire to partner with humans and share the wisdom that comes naturally to them.

The wisdom they share with clients each time they step into the round pen is mind blowing. They continually astonish me with their ability to mirror back what people are feeling in the moment. They guide us and show us a new way of being.

The power of partnering with horses as they transform and help raise the consciousness of the human species can be felt in many ways. The pure joy I feel when I am in their presence. The intimate connection I have with Spirit as I stand beside a horse and notice how our breath moves in sync. The heaviness in my heart that existed for many years has now been replaced with lightness. These are just a few of the gifts I have received.

So as I reflect back on this healing journey which began some 40 years ago, I honour the horses, as it was indeed the horses who rescued me. I now understand how powerful horses can be when it comes to healing others. I believe they were working together to heal the lost little girl who showed up at the barn all those years ago. The horses accepted me as one of their herd and took care of me. They did not see me as separate, as they know we are all connected. They were able to create the sacred space for me to begin the healing process. I never realized it at the time. All I felt was this intense pull to be near them. It all makes sense now.

I feel blessed and extremely grateful for all that horses have done for me and feel it is now my turn to pay it forward and rescue them. I hope I can spend many years providing a sacred place for horses to heal and when they are ready and willing, work in partnership with them to heal others.

Susan Collard

Susan's passion for horses spans more than four decades. Her equine experiences include both personal and professional endeavours. She first became hooked while taking a riding lesson as a young girl and eventually her love of horses led to the discovery of her soul's purpose which involved partnering with horses to assist in the personal growth and development of others.

Susan's determination to make a better life for herself and her two young sons motivated her to pursue a Psychology degree at McMaster University. After graduation, Susan was offered the opportunity to help others while working in the Career Counselling office at McMaster. Years later, the desire to understand the mind body connection as well as her keen interest in personal development, led her down another path. This path led to the completion of her Reiki 1 certification. This work seemed to fit perfectly with Susan's own healing journey and rekindled her desire to help others who were embarking on a similar journey.

Sometime later, Susan began to investigate new career opportunities and a timely encounter with a friend once again led her back to the horses. This chance encounter made her question whether it might be possible to find her soul's purpose in the healing potential of the horse human bond. Susan was accepted into a FEEL Certification program (Facilitated Equine Experiential Learning) which was the dream of merging her love of horses with the desire to improve the lives of others. Having recently purchases a rescue horse from an animal sanctuary, Susan will soon begin a lifelong partnership with Apache to help people fine their own healing path. They will be joining the herd at Meadowlark Farms, located in Copetown, Ontario where horses generously share their wisdom with humans during private FEEL sessions and workshops. Susan can be reached at collardsr@gmail.com

CHAPTER 5

You Just Don't Make That Stuff Up

By Wilma de Zeeuw

"You just don't make that stuff up," has become the expression I use most while partnering with horses to support people in their personal discovery. It blows me away every time I get the opportunity to facilitate a session or a workshop, just how precisely the horses seem to know what is needed. They behave in ways I wouldn't have believed if I had not seen it with my own eyes.

Taking you on a journey through my counselling work with the horses as the main therapists, four of my clients have allowed me to share parts their story (all identifying information has been changed) to give you an idea of how profound, impactful, and down right awesome partnering with horses can be.

The horses, who definitely want you to know them by their real names, well they are just thrilled that these stories are being told.

Let me start my introducing myself, my personal connection to horses, and how I was introduced to their tremendous healing and transformative powers.

Growing up in a small town in the Netherlands, I spent a lot of my spare time riding my bike down narrow winding roads on top of dikes, surrounded by fields with grazing cows, sheep, and of course horses. I would park my bike along the fence, grab a handful of lush green grass, and hold up my prize to the horses. If they liked the look of what I had to offer, they would saunter over and eat from my hand. If not, I would simply throw the grass in their field (with all the other lush grass), sit down close to the fence and just watch them. Fantasizing what it would be like to ride on their backs, how we would win lots of ribbons at the shows, and giving them names.

After pleading with my parents for what seemed forever (I'm sure it felt like that for them, too), I started riding lessons when I was 6.

I was a shy, anxious kid and would often worry about what horse I would be riding and if I would be able to do what the instructor would ask of me. On the day of my weekly riding lesson, it would be impossible for me to eat breakfast or concentrate at school. I would simply be too nervous to do anything but think and worry about my riding lesson. I would arrive at the barn, sweaty palms and heart beating loudly in my chest and walk over to the instructor to hear which horse I would be riding. Depending on the answer my nervousness would either increase or decrease. Then I was off to get my horse ready, brushing, cleaning their hooves, getting saddle and bridle on, all the while talking and singing to them. The lesson would always be good, but the most fun I had was always the lesson where back in their stall I would spend hours brushing, braiding their mane, feeding them hay, and sitting on the stall floor watching them eat.

Back at home after my lesson I would keep my riding clothes and boots on and would practice what I had learned on my bicycle. Rising trot, canter, serpentines, 20 meter circles and all the complex dressage moves I could think of. After dinner I would go up to my room, get out my sketchpad and draw all the different horse breeds or I would play with My Little Ponies.

If it involved a horse, real or otherwise, I was there.

As a teen I stopped riding. A combination of having a boyfriend and giving up because I deemed myself not good enough (as in not Olympic material).

The admiration for these amazing animals remained however. Volunteering at local horse shows as a scribe for judges and occasionally riding at my aunt's place.

Horses have been part of my family's history as well. My maternal grandfather was part of the Dutch Cavalry and worked the land with big Belgian draft horses. My aunt and one of her sons (my cousin) are the only ones in the family besides me who caught the horse bug.

While in university I couldn't afford to pay for riding lessons. All the money available to me went to tuition, rent, groceries, and of course, going out with my friends.

After graduating and getting my first real job as a behavioural scientist, I made a few attempts to get back in the saddle, with one attempt landing me in the ER after becoming unseated during a trail ride in the forest. I also couldn't find a barn where I felt at home. What was missing was the joy of just being around horses. All the smells and sounds; hay, grass, smell of their coat, even horse poop smells good to me (I know a little weird), the knickers, snorts, chewing, and the dunking of hay in their water bowls like we would dunk a cookie in our milk. All so wonderful and intensely happy making to me, but what I found instead were barns where the horses were true working horses, solely there to serve humans and satisfy their pursuits.

Fast forward five years and you will find me in New Zealand. Following my heart and the man I loved, got me to the other side of the world. I met Chris in a bar in the Netherlands while out with some of my friends. He was funny, smart, (he's an aerospace engineer; I know, imagine falling in love with a rocket scientist) and very exotic, as he's Canadian. I fell head over heels in love, gave up my career, and set off into the sunset.

Once I got to the other side of the world, reality started to sink in. Here I was literally on the other side of the planet without my family and friends or anything else that was familiar and comforting to me. It took me a few months to find work and as much as I was excited about this new adventure, it was also a challenge to adapt and love my new life.

Remembering what brought me comfort in the past, what had been an anchor for me growing up, led me back to the horses. Less shy but still a tad bit self conscious I decided to rekindle my love for horses. I now had the money, time, and access to horses once again. It took a while to find a place that would teach adults who don't own their own horse how to ride. Horse riding is so accessible in New Zealand, you learn how to ride on the pony parked in your backyard and go from there. My instructor who became a great friend told me stories of how she would ride her pony to school. He would graze in a field besides her school and they would ride back home together after school. How awesome is that!

The place I found in New Zealand was truly a slice of paradise. It was tucked behind this great big hedge and as soon as you came around the corner you could see big fields with horses happily grazing away amidst the rolling hills. A simple outdoor riding ring and a few stalls completed the place.

All the riding lessons happened outside, with most of it in the fields. I learned to jump by practising over fallen trees and steering by maneuvering past tree stumps. However, the best rides we had were going out into the neighbours' fields (with his permission), galloping up hills and through herds of cows, who would sometimes run along beside us.

This place, the horses and the people became my sanctuary. They were an anchor for me while I was figuring out life in New Zealand. I felt supported and at peace when I was with the horses and they certainly helped me manage the stress I was experiencing in my work as a therapist working with youth who had sexually offended others.

As much as I valued the work I did with these youth, emotionally it wasn't always easy. A lot of intense hours were spent listening to very sad, hurtful stories. Most of these youth had given up caring about themselves a long time ago and when you don't care about yourself, you often don't care about others and bad things happen. Helping them heal while holding them responsible for their actions and preventing future victimization was the name of the game.

For me this meant that by the time Friday afternoon rolled around I often felt stressed, drained, and sometimes angry or frustrated from my week at work. I would drive past that hedge, go around the corner, and drive straight to the stalls where my friend would be waiting for me with lunch. I would eat lunch with her and after lunch she would hand me a pitch fork and a wheel barrow and off I went, picking up poop in the paddocks (smaller sectioned off parts of a bigger field). After an hour or so I would calm down, the horses would move closer, and we would have a little chat, while I was sobbing in their necks. After that was done, they would usually follow me back to the barn at which point I would get my horse ready for my lesson.

I started noticing that at times when there was no time for me to emotionally offload before riding, it would affect my ride. The horse would be tense, spook easily, stop or speed up seemingly out of nowhere. Sometimes it would go so horribly wrong I would fall off. After a few of these experiences a light bulb went on, and I started to realize the horse was trying to tell me something. I thought I just needed to reassure them that I wanted to be there, with them. Ignoring with all my might the sadness, frustration, and anger I was feeling about being stuck on the other side of the world, far away from family and friends with this really complex job that I wasn't sure I liked or was even good at.

So, I just pretended harder that I was ok. However, this strategy did not work. If anything it made things worse. The only thing that seemed to work was to tell them how I was really feeling. Speaking out loud had another advantage as well. I was no longer holding my breath. You have to breathe when you talk and gradually I started to relax. Things started to flow, but as soon as my mind would wander, something unpredictable would happen, like a spook or a speeding up or slowing down. I finally figured out the horses were teaching me about being real. They were inviting me to be present in the moment, being in touch with my thoughts and my emotions.

In my work as a therapist, I had often met clients who are unaware of their thoughts, emotions, and personal boundaries or flat out lie about how they are doing.

The agency I was working for at the time, incorporated wilderness-based therapy into their program. I got to see, firsthand, the power of experience. The metaphors solicited from direct experience were so powerful for the clients that they got more healing work done in a week than they would be able to do in months of group talk therapy. It's easier to keep up an appearance, to others and yourself, if you sit in a group for 1.5 hours at a time. Not so easy to do when you are out in the bush 24 hours a day for 7 days. As a therapist these trips were brutal, but so worth it for the clients.

While being encouraged by the transformative power of direct experience in my work life and my personal relationship with the horses; I wondered how powerful the wildnerness-based therapy would be in relation with horses?

At that time I was working with a young man with a horrendously traumatic background and developmental delay. I was wondering what would happen if he were to interact with the horses? Would they be able to mirror for him, his internal state? Help him put his thoughts into words? Because talk therapy was clearly not addressing his needs, I drafted a little program for him to try working with the horses. We never got there due to circumstances, but it paved the road for me to find out more about partnering with horses in this way. A different way than happens in therapeutic riding, but no less powerful.

While pondering all of this life went on. My husband and I decided to enter a new adventure and put down roots in Canada.

Remembering my struggles of settling into a new country, I made finding a barn and reconnecting with horses my first priority after arriving in Canada.

It was there I met my now close friend Deborah, and we discovered we shared the vision of wanting to partner with horses to help people heal emotionally.

When we started looking, we found lots of different ways of working with horses in the counselling, therapy, and learning context, and we took a few mainstream courses. However we didn't find a good fit until we attended a weekend workshop at Horse Spirit Connections with Wendy Golding. After that weekend there was no going back.

For the first time in my life I felt so absolutely and completely connected to myself. That part of me that knows who I am and what I need to do to clear blocks and embrace life. I felt free from doubt, hesitation, shame, guilt, and all the other stuff that prevents us from embracing life fully.

I knew direct experience and the metaphors that go with it are powerful in generating lasting change, but this experience with the horses was kicking it up a notch.

In their presence I was able to experience my own courage and grace. In connection with the horses I experienced respect not only for them but for myself. The sense of feeling felt, felt by them but more surprising to me, feeling "me," all of me, was both mind blowing and transformative.

Needless to say that the experience of this first workshop far exceeded my expectations of what is possible in connecting with horses and people.

I had found a tangible way in which I can support people to access their own healing power. This approach is so incredibly powerful that it left me speechless and with a committed desire to learn how to facilitate this work for others.

In November 2011, I started working with the horses and FEEL teaching team, allowing me not only to hone my skills as a facilitator of this work, but also to continue to expand my self awareness, breaking down barriers, increasing trust and confidence in myself. Together with the herd I dared to gallop into the unknown. No words can express how grateful I am to the horses and the awesome people I get to call my teachers, mentors, colleagues, and friends. The little girl I once was who was so interested and in tune with horses, finally returned. It felt (and still feels) like returning home, being whole and complete again.

In May 2012 I proudly graduated from the FEEL Practitioner training, with my fresh new certificate in hand and eager to take this work out into the world.

Not having my own farm, or horses for that matter, could have made it really hard to find a barn to do this work out of; however, it's always interesting to me how things can fall into place seamlessly. I found Tranquil Acres Inc. just outside the city of Ottawa through a recent connection I had made in my network. I had moved to a new city, knowing no one besides my husband and my new baby boy.

Being around horses had provided me with the needed support and opportunities to develop new friendships in the past and so it was only logical to me that I would find a barn and let the magic of horses infuse my life once more.

I started volunteering with a stable who offers therapeutic riding lessons. After one such lesson I approached the instructor and asked her if they had thought about tapping into the horses' natural ability to support people with their emotional healing. After a few meetings with them explaining a bit more about what I meant, they suggested I contact Ryan Theriault, owner of Tranquil Acres Inc. He had just opened a therapeutic equestrian facility not too far from Ottawa and it sounded perfect.

The joint vision of supporting people and horses by respecting both species was clear from our first meeting. I had found this place where in the company of like-minded people I got the opportunity to create with the horses this sacred space of possibility, this place where we get to see beyond perceived boundaries and limitations, a place where we take flight and shape our lives.

Ryan has allowed (and continues to allow) me to use his facility and work with his beautiful herd of horses assisting clients as they courageously dive into the unknown and surface with a renewed sense of self.

Ashley

One such client is Ashley. She graciously agreed to help me out with my practice sessions while I was going through my certification program.

Ashley is a young vibrant woman, who is interested in holistic health, personal growth, and has a love for horses.

She was the first person I practised with and at that time I was still skeptical myself about this work. Even though I had experienced firsthand the impact, my rational mind was still catching up and told me things like "that only happens at Horse Spirit Connections," you have no idea what you are doing, these horses don't know what they're doing, etc.

However, I allowed myself to practice the activities with the horses the way we were taught in our training program and was able to silence the critical voice in my head just long enough to believe my eyes, trust my intuition, and validate that the horses were enjoying this way of being and interacting with humans.

The session with Ashley that stands out for me the most is her last session. She had been working with the horses for three weeks at that point and started the session while doing a little guided meditation, the intention she set for her session was to overcome the blocks that were keeping her from moving forward in her life. The horse that chose to work with her (as the horses often decide who will be the best teacher) was Mambo. Mambo is a very wise, kind, gentle soul, comfortable around people's grief and sadness.

Ashley built her obstacle course while Mambo watched her from the other side of the arena. Ashley chose the door leading out to the paddock to symbolize her new life, the place she wanted to get to. What happened next can only be described as magical, as "you just don't make that stuff up."

Ashley led Mambo towards her first obstacle, they stood there together for a little while, and Ashley proceeded to move forwards. Mambo, however stood still. Ashley tried to entice him but he wouldn't budge. She looked over at me for help. She said he was done with this obstacle. I said that I was wondering if Mambo was trying to tell her she wasn't quite there yet, that there was more stuff sitting inside connected to this obstacle. Mambo licked and chewed as I was speaking these words (licking and chewing while doing this work is an affirmation from the horses that you are speaking, thinking, or feeling truth and you are being congruent, that your outside world matches your inside world). Ashley stood a little longer at the obstacle, speaking softly to Mambo and then together they moved on. The same pattern repeated itself with each obstacle, Mambo giving clear feedback to Ashley about the releasing of the blocks. Together they walked towards the door. By this time it was lunch time for the horses and Mambo's herd mates were calling to Ryan for their hay. Ryan had asked if I had a problem with him feeding the other horses while we were in session, and I had told him I had no problem with that. I began however to get second thoughts. If Mambo wanted to he could walk right past Ashley and go for his share of the hay. I felt concern for my client, and was starting to doubt the whole process. As I was thinking all these thoughts and feeling all these feelings, Mambo remained by Ashley's side. A few times he looked over his shoulder at me as if to say, "Calm down and trust the process." Ashley and Mambo stood in that doorway for 20 minutes. She spoke to him about her doubts, she sobbed in his neck, they took big breaths together and eventually he rested his big beautiful head on her shoulder. They stood together in that connection for a few more minutes before they started walking through the doorway together. Their movement started at the exact same time, they stopped a few meters outside of that doorway at the exact same time. Ashley thanked Mambo, their connection came to a close, and Mambo walked a few metres. I joined Ashley and we debriefed her experience. The profound shift she had felt in her body, her energy, and her thoughts transcended words but was noticeable in her posture. She stood straighter, like a weight had been lifted. Mambo did not move away until our debrief was complete, and Ashley and I made our way back to the barn.

As a therapist it is my experience that it can take a long time for people to gain insight, release past hurt, and create new possibilities for themselves if all you are doing is talking about things. As much as it's helpful and useful to speak things out loud, it takes a lot of courage to open up to another human being about your inner most truth and that's taking into consideration you are consciously aware of what that is. The next brave move is to allow for connection between thoughts and feelings to occur. Initially this can be an uncomfortable and sometimes down right scary place to be.

Now, enter the horse into this equation, these beautiful beings are naturals at tuning into non- verbal communication, which includes all our thoughts and feelings. They tune into the stuff we try to hide from ourselves and others. They gently, nonjudgementally allow us to explore the crevices of our soul, of our being. Completely safe and sheltered they embrace us, all of us. Ever so gently they hand us pieces of ourselves to look at. To tenderly hold them up so light can shine in, warming the sore spots, infusing them with love. Giving us a felt sense in our bodies and our minds (not just our minds) of what it is like to release and let go. To move from what you know to what is possible to know.

It's this felt sense in your body that contributes to lasting change, because now not only your mind but also your body knows, and the body remembers. We all recall how we felt when we first fell in love (with a person, a place, a pet, a job or anything). We know how it feels to ride a bike. And riding a bike is vastly different than talking about riding a bike. That's what the work with the horses brings, the sense of riding a bike rather than talking about it. You know how it feels, to experience change rather than talking about doing something different.

That day Mambo missed out on all the hay that was there for lunch (don't worry Ryan made sure he got some). Now what horse would do that? A horse who is engaged in his role as teacher and healer that's who!

Mambo enjoying some lush grass

Shola and Wilma sharing a kiss

Wilma receiving a big hug from Monroe

Wilma savoring the moment

I got in touch with Ashley a year later and she described her sessions with the horses as one of the most empowering experiences in her life. She was able to move through some big changes thanks to the work with the horses.

I've watched Mambo support many clients over the years and he never ceases to amaze me with the depth of his compassion for the people he works with. What is striking to me about that is that Mambo had been treated unkindly by humans up until his arrival at Tranquil Acres. As an ex- racehorse he was trained harshly, being beaten every time he would do something wrong in the eyes of his trainers. He injured himself severely piercing his hip with a fence pole while trying to jump it to get away from other horses and was left to fend for himself in a paddock with not enough grass and very little water. When he got to Tranquil Acres he was underweight, had rain rot (a skin condition), and was blind in one eye.

The scars of this harsh treatment are still visible on his physical body; the place where the pole pierced him, the bald spots on his coat from the rain rot, and his blind left eye.

In my human experience these would form the perfect ingredients to be distrusting of humans, to be defensive, and possibly aggressive towards them.

Mambo however, quickly became comfortable in his new surroundings, enjoying the lush grass, hay, plenty of water and human attention.

There is so much for us humans to learn about the horse's ability to simply be, to live in the moment, and to objectively interpret experience as it happens. Not holding on to the past, not trying to control the future, simply to live and respond as the moment requires. Mambo quickly let us know he was ready for his new role as teacher and healer expressing a strong preference to work one on one with clients, gravitating towards people who struggle with sadness, grief, and depression. He would show us by galloping towards the gate as soon as a client would drive onto the parking lot, letting us know he had wisdom he wanted to share with this person.

At times when we have groups that come to us, Mambo will stay far away, too much intense energy for his liking, content to stay grazing in the field letting others of his herd be the teachers that day.

John

John came to see me after he had lost his wife. She had died unexpectedly in a car accident a few months earlier, and John was devastated. He wasn't coping and had taken an extended leave of absence from work. His friends had suggested FEEL to help him process this profound loss. John had always loved animals so he wanted to see if his animal friends could help him feel whole again. Mambo had chosen to work with John and John had chosen Mambo. There was something about Mambo John said. He couldn't quite put his finger on it, but he felt Mambo understood. During this particular session, the three of us were in the arena as I was taking John through a guided meditation to allow him to set his intention. John said, "I want my heart to feel warm again." Mambo had been watching John from the other side of the arena and as soon as John spoke these words I watched Mambo move forward with purpose towards John inhaling deeply. Mambo stopped in front of John, placed his nose on John's heart and exhaled a deep, loud breathe. It wasn't only audible; we could see it, forming a cloud in the air.

John was quite perplexed about what had just happened as he didn't expect such a literal reaction from Mambo. His heart did actually feel warm again.

In the session debrief, John spoke about feeling like his heart was no longer broken into a million pieces. The experience with Mambo made him realize he could open his heart again, that it was ok for him to love and be loved and to embrace life. That session was a turning point for John. It allowed him to slowly mourn the loss of his wife and to start to live again. We didn't need to have any more sessions after this one. Mambo's heart breath formed the catalyst John needed to access his inner wisdom, to connect with what he needed to do to heal himself.

John kept coming to the farm to just hang out with the horses, and Mambo in particular. Later on John started riding lessons. Mambo again his patient partner and teacher. Today John is full of life. They continue their friendship and partnership with Mambo willingly and patiently carrying John on his back. Time spent at the farm leaves John with the knowledge he belongs, he's worthy, and life is worth living. Pretty powerful feelings at times when you feel lonely.

Working with people like John and Ashley reminds me of why I chose this profession in the first place. We all deserve to live life to our fullest potential, but life can throw us curveballs and things happen that require healing. The invitation to allow ourselves to be restored back to wholeness so we can resume our life with confidence, and sometimes for the first time, directing our life in alignment with who we truly are is what drives me to do the work that I do.

Being a part of this sacred journey of a person's life, is both an honour and a privilege and to be partnering with horses as we co-facilitate this process for people is amplifying the amount of support and possibility for release of the old and embracing the new. Personally as a facilitator I feel immensely supported to share the responsibility of creating and holding space for my client with them. The sense that I'm not doing this alone and to be able to look at them for guidance as to whether or not I'm understanding my client, keeps me present and in the moment, with my only concern being my client, the horses, and the current experience.

As I was spending more and more time with the horses, honing my skills, increasing my own awareness and consciousness I grew more confident that I was hearing and interpreting their behaviour for clients correctly.

I started adding more FEEL workshops as well as individual sessions to my work week and so enjoy going to my "office" to watch the transformation in my clients' lives take place. After doing this for a while and finally feeling like I was getting the hang of it, the horses decided I was up for a new challenge.

Rose

Meet Rose, a confident, well-educated woman who grew up around horses, rides and owns her own horse. She had heard about FEEL, and was curious, and a little skeptical about the whole thing. She enjoyed her first session but was unsure if it was actually making a difference in her life. However, she could see how it could help others and was really looking at our sessions as a way to assess if she wanted to pursue getting trained in this modality.

Rose did a lot of talking in those first few sessions. We would be in the field and she would talk, just about anything. The more she spoke, the farther away from her the horses were. They would let her come close and be petted by her but never raised their heads to smell her or make eye contact. This behaviour from the horses is an indication for me that the person is not being present in the moment. Speaking can be a great distraction, keeping us from our real thoughts and feelings. Horses, however, still sense what's going on for us internally, even if we're not aware.

After a few sessions practising deep breathing and guided meditations, Rose increased her ability (or tolerance) to be present. The horses started to come closer and one day while setting her intention for that day's session, Rose was able to say that she was feeling sadness about how she was being treated by one of her friends. She spoke about the incident and expressed how it made her feel. As she was sharing her story, the horses moved closer and within minutes she was surrounded by five of our horses. Like a star they stood all facing her, their noses about half a metre away from her body. Necks relaxed, heads low, eyes softly closed, breathing slowly. I stepped back giving Rose and the horses space; physical as well as emotional and spiritual space.

Rose allowed for tears to flow, for sadness, anger, and defeat to rise and for those feelings to flow out of her body. She made way for powerful thoughts and answers to rise from deep within, to speak them with her voice, out loud for the first time. Rose was pleasantly surprised she had her own answers; the sense of empowerment this gave her was palpable.

In our debrief Rose described she felt a deep connection to herself and the horses.

In the next breath I said, "Well I could come and work with you and your horse at your place if you like."

It was one of those moments where you go "who said that? Did I just say that,"all the while wanting to look over your shoulder or up at the heavens to identify who just took your voice and spoke.

After I was done freaking out about it, I decided to trust whatever was going to unfold. So, when Rose called to book an appointment I meditated and connected with Rose's horse Midnight.

I knew nothing about Midnight besides her name and felt pretty self conscious about "connecting" energetically, but hey, I had learned about these things in my training and had been reading the proof and explanations about such connections in the literature to satisfy my rational mind.

When I showed up for our appointment Rose and Midnight were waiting for me. As I parked my car and opened my door I could hear giggling and when I looked over I watched Rose being pulled along by Midnight who was confidently walking in my direction. Rose commented and said she was surprised Midnight wanted to come see me at the parking lot as usually she doesn't want to go there because of farm equipment that's parked there and she gets spooked. Midnight stopped right by my side and locked her eye on me. I looked back at her and felt my heart feel warm. I told Rose Midnight and I had been talking. Midnight licked and chewed when I spoke those words (oh my, you just don't make that stuff up). A little perplexed from what had just transpired we started walking together to the arena in which we would be working. I told Rose that I wasn't sure how this would all unfold as it was my first time working with Midnight and at a different location.

I decided to re-establish my connection with Midnight first and formed what is known as a heart connection. By visualizing breathing out through your heart, sending a gentle invitation to the horse expressing your desire to connect with them, the energy fields merge and synergy gets created. To Rose, Midnight appeared aloof. She had her back turned towards me and was nibbling some grass. To me however I could see Midnight still had her eye locked on me. The more I allowed myself to be present, the easier it became to breathe through my heart. Within a few minutes Midnight stood by me with her nose on my chest. Together we basked in this connection for a while and I asked her what she wanted Rose to know. Midnight had called me here (obviously) now what did she want me to do.

As it turned out Midnight wanted her owner to know she was good enough. Underneath the confident, well-spoken exterior, Rose felt unsure about her ability to connect. Connect with people, connect with her horse, and ultimately with herself. We spent plenty of sessions exploring these topics with Midnight guiding the sessions. Every time Rose was able to let go of thoughts (be in her head) and connect with her body and feel, Midnight would come closer and stand by Rose, head relaxed, eyes slightly closed, licking and chewing.

Midnight is no longer with us but continues to inspire me to teach people about the way of the horse. Showing others what life can be like when we embrace our inner most truth and listen to the wisdom that's hidden within. The freedom it creates when we allow ourselves to be all that we are, all of it, including our shadow side.

The image I see when I think of her is Midnight galloping across the field, restricted by nothing, fully engaged in the moment. That's what it's like to be more horse like, and that's what I strive for in my life, and for those lessons I am so very grateful.

Sylvia

My last story is that of Sylvia. She was told about FEEL by a family friend who suggested she try it to build her confidence. Sylvia felt she needed to do this (build her confidence) as she was in her mid twenties but still single and she should have had a boyfriend by now. At one particular session we entered the paddock where five of our horses were having their afternoon hay. Sylvia froze as we entered the paddock. All the horses looked up at her, than turned away and continued eating their hay. I invited Sylvia to connect to her breath and start breathing slowly and deeply. As she did this, she was able to share what was going on for her. She made the comparison to entering a party alone and not knowing anyone. Sylvia was overcome with worry on how to behave and froze in response. Will they like me? Why are they ignoring me? Should I behave differently? These were all questions that were brought to the surface as she stood in the paddock with the horses. Sylvia expressed she felt like she needed to be somebody else, somebody more outgoing, prettier, or smarter. The horses remained stuck with their faces in the hay. I asked her, "Who are you?" Connect to your breath, visualize your heart opening and connecting to the horses' hearts, allow for the words to come.

We had been practising this heart connection exercise a few times and Sylvia was able to open her heart and connect with the horses.

When she spoke next her posture changed. She stood straighter, smiled, and said she was kind, gentle, and loving.

The horses stopped their grazing and all moved towards her. I noticed Monroe looking at her and asked her to turn her attention to him and ask what his message was for her. With tears streaming down her face she said, "The horses see my soul. I don't have to be anyone but me. They love me and I can love me."

Now, let me tell you a little bit about Monroe. He's tall, dark, and handsome, with a big personality. Monroe is the herd leader and takes great pride in keeping everybody safe. He's the horse that people notice first because of his regal presence, and he's also the horse people often feel intimidated by. He teaches people about personal space and boundaries as he will try and nibble you with his big horse lips if you don't hold your own. If he were a person, he would be that boy in high school everyone had a crush on. The one that makes you lose your voice and reduces you to a trembling, blushing mess. How interesting he would be the one "talking" to Sylvia about loving herself.

Ultimately Monroe teaches people to love and honour themselves and their talents the way he does his own. He invites people to do this without shame or excuse, with an open heart, and with their ego in check. He teaches us that we don't serve the world by playing small and that embracing our whole self includes our beauty, our talents, and our awesomeness. Embracing all the good stuff about ourselves can sometimes be harder than admitting the not-so-great parts. Yet, when we do, we get a glimpse of who we truly are and it becomes a whole lot easier to align ourselves with what we need to do in this lifetime.

This particular session formed a turning point in Sylvia's life. She realized she had been looking for a boyfriend because she thought she had to. All her friends had, and so she felt that she needed to live up to the expectation of being in a relationship. This session made her realize she did not want to date at this point in time and allowed her to focus on what was important to her. She focused on her career, hobbies, and planned to take a big trip oversees the next summer.

Sylvia still comes to the farm for the occasional session at times when she needs a reminder to stay on her life's path. Monroe continues to be a barometer for her in terms of how far she has allowed herself to get off track. At one of our last sessions I watched on as Sylvia walked into the paddock to greet Monroe. He looked up, walked a few steps towards her, and waited with his head held high for her to approach. With only a metre between them Sylvia stopped and looked at Monroe. Monroe wanted to step towards her but Sylvia told him with her body language to stay put, which he did. Sylvia smiled a big smile from ear to ear, it was an affirmation for her of how far she has come in establishing boundaries and personal space, with love and grace, without the need to apologize for them. Sylvia moved towards Monroe and started stroking him, Monroe returned the favour and started nibbling her hair ever so gently. It was beautiful for me to watch this tender connection between two souls, completely engaged with each other and in the moment.

These are just some of the stories I've had the privilege to witness, and every FEEL Practitioner I speak with has a ton more of equally amazing "You just don't make that stuff up" stories to add.

When in the presence of these like-minded people, my heart glows, and I'm proud to be part of this community.

The world and its people are in desperate need of healing, balance, and belonging. Creating and contributing to a world in which horses, who have stood alongside man all throughout history, are finally being acknowledged for their incredible wisdom as teachers and healers is both humbling and exciting.

Horses have formed a constant in my personal life and in the last few years in my work life as well. Personally the work with the horses has allowed me to know things about myself I had no idea possible. Working with them as my teachers has made me want to be a more authentic version of myself. It has allowed me to look at my role as mother, daughter, partner, friend, and professional.

In my role as a therapist and life coach, partnering with the horses has allowed me to connect with clients who needed something different than I was able to offer with more traditional in-office sessions. The sense of feeling felt, of creating new experiences that slowly replace the old ingrained reactions, happens almost automatically when we work with the horses.

The empowerment that comes from being able to recognize what your body is trying to tell you through its emotions and integrating this into a response rather than a reaction to a situation is incredibly powerful to a person and for me as a therapist, it's that experience for a client that makes my heart sing and affirms that this is what I'm supposed to do with my life.

From the horses and from me, I wish you love, light, and courage on your journey through life. Our past does not need to define our future, and the present is where we can start to shape the future we desire for ourselves.

The horses are calling. Will you answer their call...

Much gratitude

Wilma de Zeeuw

Wilma de Zeeuw

Wilma de Zeeuw, holds a Masters degree in Social Sciences, specializing in behavioural and family problems, from Radboud University in Nijmegen the Netherlands. This degree formed the foundation for her work, which has taken her to three different countries and various government and community adolescent mental health agencies.

While living and working in New Zealand, Wilma explored more holistic ways to support her own healing and development, and looked for ways to bring this approach to her clients. Soon, Wilderness Therapy, Reiki and breathing exercises became standard options for her clients.

In addition to incorporating alternative healing modalities within her counselling practice, Wilma became a Certified FEEL Practitioner to add her work with horses to support her clients. She is incorporating new ways in which horses can support human growth and development. Wilma facilitates her clients in a way they can experience the transformative impact of experiential learning through the gentle healing presence of horses.

Wilma completed the FEEL Practitioner program in 2012 and has been offering private sessions as well as group workshops out of Tranquil Acres Inc. located in Ottawa,Ontario ever since.

The horses and the clients she has the privilege to work with, affirm time and time again the importance of authentic connection with ourselves and others to find what we seek to heal and evolve in our lives. For more information about Wilma's counselling programs, please visit: www.counsellingwithwilma.ca

CHAPTER 6

The Invitation

By Andre Leclipteux

In Balance

Today, the dawn of a new day
When men help seed a new balance

Birthed by women who rekindled their power
Quietly standing holding a new light

Grounded in the earth and shooting for the sky
A heart of gratitude seeking forgiveness

Let us spread our wings on the winds of change
To create a balance within ourselves

To fully express ourselves as human be-ings
Creating a new reality rooted in compassion

So our children and their children and their children
Will praise us in years to come

As a new dream is birthed from the edge of waste
Into a harmonious song that resonates beyond

A new vibration to change the pattern of yesterday
That cycles outwards and meets a new day

Embracing a new energy that creates our movement
An evolution into the light

To be witnessed with our mind
Felt in our heart
And embraced by our spirit,
Our soul.

Since 2006 my partner Wendy Golding and I have invited and facilitated a great number of women and men, of all ages to experience the 'horse work.' At Horse Spirit Connections we've conducted small-group workshops, welcomed at-risk-youth, designed corporate team-building days, and provided one-on-one intensives to a variety of people wanting to experience the transformational opportunities presented by the horses. As a FEEL Practitioner I have the honour of designing, managing, and witnessing their experiences.

Our horses have an innate ability to sense, resonate, and respond to our energy. Not just our words but all of what we present to them. It's as if they have access to our subconscious and they begin to answer a question before the question is asked or formed in our psyche or outwardly expressed. The magic reveals itself when these thoughtful creatures with limited forms of expression mirror and communicate back to us.

Carlos Castenada in his writing on the teachings of Don Juan referred to a time when man had 'Silent Knowledge'[1], the ability to know deep within without attaching thoughts or words nor having the need to express it. Using the Mayan calendar as reference, I'm guessing this would be a time that existed more than 5,500 years ago. As man evolved he reached the 'Place of Reason' where he used his mind to make sense of his world. His Ego needing to understand, control, dominate, and power over everything he saw, touched, and experienced.

The horse's evolution is very different.[2] Physically they have changed very little over the millions of years that they too have been on this earth. They may be a little taller, shorter, or stockier yet their inner survival and communication skills have been unchanged. Gut instinct, horsepower, and horse sense are all terms which honour the horse's gifts. History has repeatedly shown that the horse was and is a gift to humans.

The idea of sharing stories of how the horse continues to be a gift to us was the seed that quickly birthed itself into this book. When invited to participate, or should I say when my wife strongly suggested that I participate, my immediate reaction was to shut down and turn off the lights! What did I have to say that others hadn't already said? I firmly believe the 'horse work' is something you need to experience, to feel it in your body, not something to be dredged, dissected, and put on the wall for others to critique! After a night of horses presenting themselves in my dreams, I awoke with a clearer yet inquisitive mind and on the way to the barn, I opted to ask the horses for their help and guidance. In the silence, Spirit Walker, one of our 12 horses came to mind.

Spirit Walker (not his birth name) typifies the horse racing industry. As a thoroughbred he was bred to race and born to be more. He did well in his first year on the track, fair to say he most likely returned his owners investment. In his second year, he didn't show the same promise and as he slipped from placing so did his fate. Discarded, undernourished, and without purpose he became the victim of an old mindset that regards horses as nothing but a tool, life without consciousness, property to do with what one wishes.

Fate did cross his path as he and several others were scooped up at the horse rescue, loaded into a trailer for a cross-country ride to different pastures and purpose. Still embodying the victim, his new owner found him lacking speed, presence, and having soft feet. His opportunity for a new life was slipping.

When he arrived at Horse Spirit Connections he was 5 years old, shy and timid, unsure of himself. The other horses wanted nothing to do with him as if the word "victim" was painted on his side in loud gutter found graffiti. We changed his racing name to "Buddy" and gave him time to heal.

Buddy was the ideal name for him at that time for he was looking for a best friend, and he knew how to welcome you into his space. When I entered the barn he would raise his head over the stall, his ears first appearing, followed by his nostrils flaring, working overtime to detect who was approaching. He would let out a soft rolling snicker, asking who was there, stating a desire to be acknowledged, and sending an invitation to play.

I love feeding the horses their grain in the morning. It's a time to bond, to feel purposed, to be of service. As I come around the corner with six buckets individually marked and holding the promise of a satisfied stomach, Buddy would snort, a loud proclamation of excitement, anticipation, and thanks. This magnificent horse was rendered the size of a puppy nervously sitting still, fully recoiled to execute a command for a measly prize. His young belly joyful at the anticipation, the promise of a meager satisfaction would be vocalized louder than a whisper, softer than a scream, and trembling at the remembrance of starvation. And I wonder if over time his feeling of emptiness will fade or will the memory of hunger remain.

Buddy evolved from being turned out alone, to being in a small herd with our eldest horse Monty and our youngest Aria. It was all part of a process that allowed him to be a horse again, to be with his own kind, to explore and express himself as a horse with minimal human intervention, to create and hold a space for his own healing without the hindrance of human expectations and judgment. Eighteen months later I was looking at a new horse. He was standing tall and proud within a larger herd. His dark brown coat shining by the light of the day reflected his youthful and muscular physique. Getting excited his tail would almost stand on end flying high and putting Arabians to shame. He had found his stride.

As this magnificent being was introduced to the FEEL 'horse work' he would choose people that he wished to work with. Seeing the spark in his eye we knew he was taking them on a journey, a spiritual journey of discovering who they were. Observing from the sidelines, the time was right; he had shed his old cloak and was stepping into being "Spirit Walker."

I invited him to a new activity, the Reflective Round Pen, telling him it would be the two of us. Deep down I believe he already knew what was being asked and how to do it. Our horses have repeatedly shown us the power of the horse consciousness. When we introduce a concept or new activity to a couple of horses it impacts the collective consciousness of the herd and before long they demonstrate to us that they all know the exercise and get it. This training model is incredibly efficient and fast, far superior to anything I've experienced as a human!

The Reflective Round Pen is an opportunity for a human to converse with a horse at liberty in a 60-foot round pen. The process is simple. Standing outside the round pen, the participant is led through an exercise of quieting the mind, taking stock of any sensations or messages from the body, connecting with the horse through heart resonance, and in that moment going into the heart (as opposed to the mind) and asking what is it you wish to seek, ask, need to express, or have this experience represent. It's called a heart's desire and it's in the moment. Once expressed the participant then enters the round pen for an interaction with the horse.

The horse is free to be. To stand, to connect, to walk away, to approach, to call out, to be a mirror reflecting back, or to use its actions as communication to the participant. Over the years I have been in awe and spellbound at the feedback shared and provided by the horses. It's as if they are tapping a well of silent knowledge and expressing in any way they can, using what limited resources they have. They have repeatedly used the same action to communicate the same thought. Licking and chewing to state their agreement with a thought or question and some nodding their agreement with their heads. Stomping their foot as a form of frustration, or to dig deeper. They will yawn, and at times repeatedly, as a way to release energy on our behalf. To communicate "being vulnerable" they will lie down, exposing their belly and sometimes roll.

They listen to us in whatever language we use: English, French, Spanish, be it verbal or non verbal. They pick up the beliefs we place on items. One of those items is "the wand" a long crop or rigid whip which holds no energy on its own and is used as an extension of one's arm. Having facilitated this work for many years, we've seen horses, and unfortunately people, respond negatively to crops and whips, a physical recoil as muscles tense at the sight or sound, and their body whispers a secret of past abuse. We teach people to use the wand to set a boundary, claim their space, and stand strong against an approaching horse if and when they are uncomfortable. We've also seen the horse pick up the wand to inform a person to be aware of their boundaries. When we overlaid native wheel teachings on the round pen, being the east represents spirit, the west represents the body, south the heart, and north the mind, it wasn't long before the horses were standing or weaving patterns using the same belief to communicate back to us "You're in your head" or "You're missing the heart." Their messages tend to be short and to the point especially in light of the limited resources available to them (so when a horse poops, turns around and smells it, it could very well be asking, "Whose crap is this?").

The more experienced horses tend to be subtle with their actions. Horses new to this work tend to be more exaggerated or explicit in their movements and actions. They seem to give it their all–the audition to end all auditions–knowing the importance of communications and a desire to be crystal clear and fully understood. And this was Spirit Walker's first Reflective Round Pen and I was to be his first participant.

Stepping in

This was a rare occasion as typically during a workshop I am one of the facilitators, not the participant. Following gut instincts, my co-facilitator and I had opted to demo the Reflective Round Pen to this group which created an opportunity for me to be the participant, and for Spirit Walker an initiation.

Standing outside the round pen, the facilitator reminds me of the process and assures me that she will guide me through the opening exercises including connecting with the horse. Spirit Walker is standing alert, taking everything in; listening to all the energies, knowing this is his new job, his new role, his new purpose. I quiet my mind and allow the world to slip away, to be fully present in the moment. The far edges of my peripheral vision begin to blur as my focus shifts away from the physically present external world. The audience, sitting no more than 30 feet from me, fades away from consciousness and their voices are rendered inaudible, turning down the volume control of my outer ear. My inner ear by comparison seems more alert, my body more receptive and my breathing has altered–slower, deeper, with more determination. I feel my center dropping into the earth, my feet firmly supporting my body. And from this place I ask for my heart's desire, what is it I wish this session to represent, what is it that I'm seeking, what is the question that my heart longs to ask?

And the words come out "What am I to write about?"

Spirit Walker has been very attentive; his ears perked up and pointed in my direction. He knows on some level that all of this is really important. Inside the round pen he stands 6 feet away, his big dark eyes locked in on me. He's motionless and when he hears my heart desires, his penis drops. This was a profound event; our male horses drop their penis when a strong heart connection has been established between the participant and the horse, so Spirit Walker was acknowledging the connection and expressing it.

Men are like the sun. What you see is what you get. There's nothing hidden, no secrets to be revealed. Spirit Walker is standing in his full pride, his full masculinity, the "victim" having been replaced by purpose and pride. He's rekindling a feeling deep down within me, the pride of youth vanished with age, beliefs locked from criticism hidden from self-scrutiny, and a near silent whisper seeking to escape and proclaim who I am. And I hear, "Write about the masculine."

My immediate response is fear! My instincts screaming denial "I didn't hear that!" and my ego mind uttering a chuckled and sarcastic "Oh yah. Sure."

In a split second my response is quickly shadowed by a childlike innocence at hearing a loud and vocal response to a silent question that no one was supposed to hear, "Where did that come from?"

And then the realization; the opening of a door deep in my unconscious; light entering a dark space; the door slowly exposing a crack of light that softly fills the whole room to reveal a thought; a treasure chest in the middle of a vast and empty room; unopened and inviting.

I feel his invitation to enter the round pen to interact and bare witness to his species' wisdom. On entering I walk to the center, take a breath to re-center myself, and open myself to the experience. I send out my invitation asking him to show me. He begins to move; walking then standing in the southeast, the place we know to be our self-concepts, our attitudes, our approaches to life, and our ancestors. Standing with determination he picks up his left front leg and digs it into the ground pulling it towards him moving the shavings and clearly drawing a line. Using his right front leg he does the same and he repeats his actions alternating between left and right legs. Normally a horse paws at the ground to show frustration, or they pound the ground to make a point, but this is different. Alternating from foot to foot, he hits the same mark, the same spot, each time and pulls back drawing a "V" in the ground.

His actions hit a chord in me, knowledge old and true. Earth medicine they call it. The left side is our feminine, our receptive side and the right is our masculine, our active side. Were, we, at one time, so balanced that the two were one? That spot that he keeps hitting so accurately with both hooves, the bottom of the "V?" And then cutting into the ground he clearly is showing how it's separated, how the point becomes a line and each line travels a different angle ending in separation.

His behavior is so out of character for any horse, my mind is racing through assumptions, scenarios, and hypothesis all at the same time, stretching for a thought that fits! Is he showing me the path that I've travelled or am travelling? Have I consciously or unconsciously allowed my masculine and feminine to slip and be out of balance? Or is he painting a bigger picture, one that exposes the separation existing or expanding farther apart between the masculine and feminine be it in relationships, our society, or exponentially, affecting humanity and the world?

Spirit Walker is now staring at me his eyes piercing me making sure I got it. And then he drops! His entire and complete body drops right to the ground!

When horses are looking for a place to roll they tend to sniff the ground looking for that ideal spot. When they find it they lower themselves carefully knowing their legs are fragile yet strong enough to hold 1,000 or more pounds of flesh and muscle. Their movement is slow as their legs shake struggling to hold their raw mass as they lower themselves. It appears as an ordeal until they finally fold their lower legs underneath them and allow gravity to take over, the final foot a gentle fall to the ground followed by a sigh of relief, a big exhale, and all the tension is gone from their body.

But for Spirit Walker, his was a determined and calculated drop from a full standing position, as if his legs had instantaneously lost their ability to hold his young muscular body. I stand in awe of his actions seeking within an understanding of what he is communicating. I fear the separation between the feminine and masculine in our society is creating a void that could be considered dangerous—for humans, horses, and the earth we inhabit. Have we in this age of reason, convinced ourselves of our importance and given our power away to fear creating entities and static objects that drain us of our life force?

The horses don't seem to work from this place of reason. They seem to operate from their hearts and continually give to us humans. Before they were domesticated they were hunted for food. Then they became our means of transportation, our machines, and our muscles to move and farm the land. They have been praised, revered, idealized, hunted, abused, and neglected, and they still stand beside us as a loyal companion, partner, and saviors. Today they are helping us on a new journey—one to find ourselves, redefine who we are, and help us evolve.

They are constantly reminding us to operate from our body, for that is the physicalness of who we are. They remind us to be present in our bodies. To take action when action is required and then go back to grazing. To live in the present moment and let go of the past and stop clinging to a future that hasn't manifested. To live in a herd which is cooperative and each member has a role and function.

And now Spirit Walker is rolling, exposing his belly, showing his full vulnerability. Horses are prey animals and are preyed upon by meat-eating animals including humans. When they expose their belly they trust in the moment that nothing is going to harm them. When they roll in front of us they are trusting the moment or reminding us to be vulnerable, to let down our guard, and experience the moment as it presents itself.

Vulnerability is being in that awkward moment when something is about to change or be revealed, when behaviors or beliefs need to be questioned. It's not a place that many find comfortable. Oddly it feels like other emotions—anger, fear, sadness. There's an adrenaline rush that comes with it, the body wanting to know if "now" is the time to fight or flight or freeze. Horses' natural tendency when facing a threat or danger is flight, to run or gallop to a place of safety and return to grazing. In contrast, men's natural tendency is fight, to confront it, size it up, control it, or defeat it, and maybe it's this visceral reflex that drives his craving for domination. And the third option is the one I am feeling—to—freeze—to allow the moment to arrive and shroud me without action or reaction, to numb the mind and senses for the unknown to be revealed. A thought begins to form and I wonder if this is Spirit Walker's message—are we, the collective "we", at a point in our human evolution that we are vulnerable? That we must make changes to our behaviors and our beliefs?

We have entered a new age—as prophesized by the Mayan and Hopi cultures—and the reality is we are still in a transitional phase. Humans cannot continue to abuse and exhaust earth's resources. Fear and greed have been the drivers for advancements, separation, exploitation, and destruction. In this age of reason we have used our minds to justify our actions, control what we can, and given ourselves power over the rest. We are the cancer that refuses to let go while killing its host. In short, we have lost our heart. We are out of balance seeking a new identity while hanging on to false beliefs and failing ideas.

We need to restore balance and to do so we must step into that place of vulnerability.

The image of the masculine has deteriorated over the last century. Linda Kohanov referred to it in the chapter "Merlin's Spirit" in her book *"Way of the Horse: Equine Archetypes for Self Discovery – A Book of Exploration"* where she states "True masculinity has been twisted, tortured, and betrayed by a culture of conquest and consumerism. It's hard to fathom what a peaceful, healthy form of virility might look like. To have any hope of changing the world, men and women must reevaluate and resocialize the active, masculine principle within their own families—and their own psyches— a task requiring significant soul-searching and imagination."[3]

Calling it the Redemption of the Masculine, she expressed the gift being "Power and gentleness find a new way to coexist, balance, and finally heal the immense injustices perpetrated by—and on—the masculine body, mind, and spirit."

A meeting of the minds
Andre and Contendor share a moment after a deep heart-connected experience

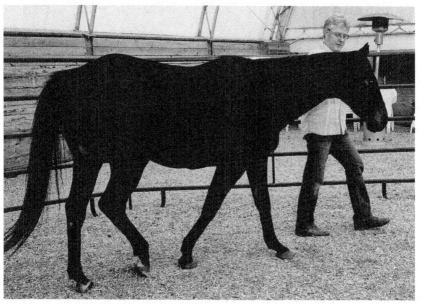

Spirit Walker following Andre as they walk together in the round pen

Spirit Walker, contemplating rolling

Spirit Walker, lying down and showing vulnerability

I believe society has stripped the male gender of their naturalness and purpose thanks in part to skewed headlines and deceitful advertising, the media promoting an impossible fictional image that mainstream adores as it reverberates exponentially with discriminatory beliefs. His self-worth is measured by material gains, judged, applauded, or condemned by others. His relationship with himself, men, women and even animals was criticized and ridiculed until he stood alone, isolated, afraid to express love of self or others. He no longer can freely express himself without being scrutinized. Society dictates what he can say and how he should act, with penalty of rejection and abandonment. His misbehavior seen as a nuisance has been rounded up like wild horses to a coral for slaughter by righteous thoughts executing and excusing themselves of barbaric deeds. The swing of this pendulum cries for individuals, mavericks in their own right to step forth and break this homogeneous mold of the masculine, daring to be a beacon of inspiration for others. I too felt seized by the demands placed by others and society, many of which were cloaked in the promise of ease, advancement, and freedom. And the horses were there, reminding me to focus on my inner journey, to be centered and grounded and glimpse at an alternative state of being.

The feminine has also gone through a transformation stepping out of the shadows to claim equality and then beginning an inner journey of self-discovery.

Spirit Walker plants his feet on the ground and in a quick move he springs up to stand on all four and begins to walk towards me his eyes fixed on mine. His quick motion breaks the silence, the rush of his energy, urgency to be noted. A few strides and he is standing in front of me, eye to eye, towering my height. And gently he lowers his head placing his forehead on my chest. I can feel my heart beating, a loud echoing series of thumps reverberating in my chest. There are no thoughts going through my head, my body feels grounded and, I have this knowing, an inner sense that this magnificent animal is helping me expand my heart and a gentle reminder to live life from the heart. My hand reaches up to touch him and he sniffs it, his big soft nostrils flaring as if to take in all of my essence.

The action of my hand prompts a memory, the need to touch, to be physical, to reach out versus seeking within. I recall my inner journey began in my late teens defining for myself what my beliefs, needs, and desires were, instead of blind acceptance to the definitions and meanings being told and sold, rules forced to follow, concepts served without question. Questions of who am I, where did I come from, why am I here. and where am I going reverberated in my ears as my uncertainty and lack of conviction in following the footsteps before me pulled me forwards. I began looking in mirrors, windows, and the spaces between being told and wanting to experience all with the determination to define the "me". The answers to the questions of what is a man, a family, love, relationships, faith, continued to be unraveled juxtaposed to what I was being told. Soon the training wheels were removed and it felt like being propelled into a fast current, a decision to swim or sink, to play the hand that was dealt, to be accepted. By my late twenties the crusade had dwindled becoming sporadic until my forties when it was rekindled with shamanism and earth medicine and the horses.

Over many years of facilitating young adults to this horse work I've observed and am amazed to discern a similar pattern. Boys in their late teens tend to be on an inner journey of self-discovery. They are more aware of their feelings, although at times not able to express it or put words to it. They are asking questions of themselves to define themselves. The girls of the same age seem to be on an outward journey having already formed cliques to define themselves. Stating what they like and dislike they dress themselves not only in the clothes but the thoughts of others. By the times both are in their late teens they're travelling an outward journey to define themselves within a material world—schooling, job, car, video games, movies, music—each a component, a patch on a quilt, or a badge they wear with pride, all to say "I am..."

It is the women who outnumber the men coming to our workshops, some attracted to the horses rekindling a long love affair, others being drawn by their intuition or attracted by a repeating question pulsing in their mind and quivering in their body. Is it bravery, curiosity, or innocence that propels them to stand on the threshold of exploration and change, a yearning percolating from behind their eyes, intuitively knowing there must be more? Over time there is a pattern that evolves and I am honoured to witness these women begin or continue their inner journey, looking for a greater image of themselves, wanting resolution to actions in their past, and seeking clarity on their life's purpose. In comparison the men seem trapped on a race track preforming mindless laps, competing for a prize never defined, collecting things to express their gains, cutting notches on their belt, keeping tabs on the experiences that have kept their bodies in a state of existence and advancement. And those daring to be seen seeking a higher purpose have a delicate hold of a candle sheltering it from the winds of change, against an onslaught of marketing assaults and peer condemnation. The horses, four feet on the ground, offer themselves as a windbreak, a solitary moment of reflection for men to explore their values, beliefs, and convictions, and reclaim their footing in the world.

Nudging me I move and start walking, my feet leading without my awareness. Spirit Walker is walking beside me letting me know that he's there supporting me. But he knows that time is of the essence and he begins to run, teasing me to do the same, to put myself into action. In his quiet yet deliberate way he's inviting to join him on a crusade to step out of an old pattern and create a new one. When my eyes fall upon him I no longer see the victim that arrived two years past. He stands majestically in the full knowing of who he is and a willingness to assist and empower others. As I walk to the exit, I feel his pride and my back arches, my shoulders straighten, I am standing taller, smiling, knowing my cup is full!

Time is a trickster. The 10 minutes with Spirit Walker has felt like an eternity, an expedition blending past, present, and future with no bearing to the tick or tock that dictates my day. Another lesson the horses like to reveal; how to be grounded in the present and disregard time. In contrast, the next 10 minutes, the second part of this exercise, has the potential to expand each second if I'm ungrounded and allow the weight of my nervousness to drag.

Stepping out of the round pen, the facilitator escorts me to one of the two chairs facing the group and asks me to share my heart's desire with the group. My mind is suddenly reminded that seven other people, all women as it turns out, have witnessed my experience and are there to offer the outward reflections, what they saw, what they felt, what they experienced. This is an incredible and valuable part of the Reflective Round Pen. It can validate inner thoughts, provide substance and depth to the experience, shine a light on what the participant could not see or was blind to see. People speak of how the experience resonated inside them, what part touched them, or which emotion surfaced for them. Sometimes there are tears of sadness that surface or tears of joy that spring from an old closed wound. Other times there's laughter that erupts to cleanse and satiate the group. They have been patiently observing, taking notes, performing mental and heart gymnastics to expose and understand the mystery they were witnessing and now they are eager to validate their subjective observations by hearing and listening to the participant as he/she shares his/her inner journey.

Spirit Walker has taken his space standing behind me. His neck reaching high above the metal round pen and curving so his head comes down to touch the top of my head. A reminder that he is still supportive, reassuring me that I am not alone, and the words come out "My heart's desire was to determine—what am I to write about?"

Sharing feedback

There is an energy that zips through the audience as each one checks their notes both written and mentally recorded, to authenticate Spirit Walker's actions and my heart's desire. Individually they begin to share:

"Even before you walked in the round pen, Spirit was right there at your back supporting you in whatever you were seeking. And when he dropped his penis I wasn't sure if he was acknowledging your heart connection with him or if it was a deep guttural instinct portraying the masculine."

"Spirit was so determined to communicate with you! When pawing at the ground I saw it was deliberate and when he dropped to roll, it took my breath away. His statement was so clear to me—to dive in, dig in, be vulnerable, and trust it."

"That horse loves you! Even now he stands behind you letting you know he's there for you. I saw the beautiful harmonious bond between the two of you. I now see and appreciate how horses are so supportive of us when we step into that place of vulnerability to do our personal work."

"After he rolled and shook, he walked directly towards you in the centre. I saw the strength in you as a man—to hold space for whatever needs to occur and be revealed.

When he touched your heart, he too touched mine and I felt it open wide and radiate with pure joy."

"It was so freeing to watch Spirit connect with you and then join up. You could have gone anywhere and he would have followed. It made me realize the power of intimacy in building strong relationships."

Their words resonate with my experience, and I can feel my inner body vibrating, a hidden tuning fork generating a higher frequency within. So much of what they saw I felt while in the Round Pen with Spirit Walker.

As I listen to their observations, their feedback, the sharing of their experiences I am reminded of the impact we have on the space and one another. I may have entered the round pen for my own benefit, my own quest and yet I became the stimulus for their journey, an inspiration to step out of normality and seek an unknown, an unfamiliar both within and outside of themselves. And it wasn't just me!

Spirit Walker, his long and purposeful strides, is circling inside the round pen, pleased to hear the positive and encouraging feedback. He returns to stand behind me letting out a joyful and inquisitive neigh. Nudging at me again, prompting me to share, to reveal my thoughts, the measure of what I gained.

The facilitator knowing the time has come, the moment of truth and revelation, inhales to breathe, the sound piercing my pregnant pause. Exploring my eyes to unlock my thoughts a silent and openhearted invitation is delivered to share with the group. Seven women sitting at the edge of their seat holding their breath as if this was the unveiling of the century, a cliff hanger to be in resonance with the unknown as it is fortold. "It was an incredible experience," I begin not knowing where to begin trusting that if one word comes out, others will follow until hidden thoughts are exposed. "I can't believe the speed and depth at which we connected and the decisiveness of his actions. To me he was emphasizing the masculine and placing a lot of attention on relationships." I look across to a succession of inquiring eyes set on me and Spirit Walker beyond. Another neigh from Spirit Walker, a challenge to endure the spotlight, to expose myself by expressing thoughts that have been sheltered, fermenting until the day is just right. And his earlier message comes back to me, "There is no more time."

I feel my heart racing, my palms sweating, a nervousness crawling and scratching at my throat, my mind exploring an empty cave for a resolution to this feeling! The years of facilitating return and thoughts begin to form. Breathe... Relax... Feel the support... Be in the moment... Be the moment... Breathe, and continue...

Stepping out

"I have long wondered about the roles of the masculine and feminine as I believe they have shifted and need to shift due to all the turmoil, confusion, and degradation that have occurred."

"People both men and women, tend to fall into three categories; asleep, awake, and aware. People who are asleep tend to be oblivious to the shifts occurring. They continue to walk by the window of change, without looking in, each step in denial as they reach out to grasp and secure their old armor. They're continuing their outward journey in hopes of defining themselves with material gains, power, and position. This is the mentality that has governed man's actions for many years spinning and weaving the world into the chaos that currently thrives. Those awake are hearing rumbles from the earth, possibly murmurs from their core, and hopefully the call of the horses. They are awakening to the idea that something is off kilter, out of alignment, that something is missing from the wholeness of who they are. They stand in the doorway peering down a corridor of uncertainty seeking answers from their mind that cannot be answered by the mind. As questions are formed and they step into a place of presence, into the doorway, I have observed the horses lined up at the gate ready to work with them, yawning to release stuck energy on their behalf. Those aware have started their inner journey towards enlightenment–whatever that light might be for them. They are breaking old patterns, eradicating outdated and stale dogma. They seek a balance within themselves and harmony within relationships.

They are engaging their imagination to open and expand their heart and spirit to a new way of being. It is here the horses have helped me the greatest; being a mirror to my own reflection, an instant biofeedback machine, a silent nudge encouraging me to move onwards and deeper."

I become consciously aware of my body position, sitting upright, engaged, breathing deeply with a strong exhale, delivering a speech from an obscure cavern recently set ablazed by the tiniest light that explodes into illumination. Facing seven women I call upon the strength of the horses, to be completely grounded, daring myself to continue.

"I see women embracing this horse work as part of their inner journey to discover themselves. There is a willingness to step in front of and look into any mirror to inspect and study the product and creation of her life. Her fearlessness might be evolving from desperation or the realization that she must be more than just a body and mind caught in the physical reality we call life. Her desire to be empowered is leading her to redefine her role on every stage she walks, strides, tackle, or sits. I believe her journey is to find her power, her inner power of heart and soul, and her destiny is to claim it."

Spirit Walker is fully alert not only to my words, tone of voice, and body language but likewise to the environment. He hears the neighs and whinnies drifting from the barn, and I'm pretty sure it's the other male horses–Thor, Redman, and Contendor–adding their voice to the mix.

"I believe the role of the masculine is to provide and hold space for the feminine so she can do her work and step into her power, protect the dream of a new reality, a higher frequency of heart and soul, our evolution as humans, so the new feminine may birth the new masculine."

A blanket of silence envelopes the group and the space, keeping the warmth of love and compassion in and the threat and sounds of fear out. I recall that sensation as a child, being tucked into bed, permitting the thoughts of the day to evaporate, welcoming the dream to reveal possibilities, empowered by trust and hope to embrace a new day.

The invitation is delivered within the silence. Spirit Walker is licking and chewing, affirming his agreement.

The back of my mind instantly converts to a movie screen with reruns of horse sessions. Thor, the gentle giant, our big black Percheron kicking his heals then majestically trotting around the pen under the command of a woman, who discovered, conjured, and channeled her power. Redman, the colorful Spotted Mountain Horse, a jokester eyeing for the right timing to deliver the punch line, does a fast switch to an overly smug man who finds himself being lunged, running in circles around a horse standing comfortably in the center, Redman having executed the perfect role reversal. Contendor, our mysterious, magical, and overly sensitive Paso Fino, stands perfectly still in the center of the round pen holding space for a woman exploring her inner scape, seeking to define herself, walks around, to and from him for 10 minutes. And Paris, our jet black Arabian Quarter Horse, locking down all four at the start of a leading exercise until the participant (regardless of sex or age) finds the balance between the feminine and masculine in their heart. All profound experiences and today, Spirit Walker has joined their rank of teacher, healer, transformational guide, and magician. The gratitude I feel comes gushing from the ground and erupts through my body, and as the wave recedes it reveals the fatherly pride I feel in my heart and shines on my face.

Spirit Walker snorts putting an exclamation on the completion of the exercise. The facilitator coughs to release the dryness in her throat and breaks the pregnant pause. "And what is your nugget, your take away, that one gem that you will carry with you as you walk this out?"

Under normal circumstances my logical brain would scream at such an insane request to take all of what has transposed and to bring it down to one short concise thought! And I recognize and am thankful that I'm not currently functioning from that turret.

"The horses are inviting us to discover ourselves in a whole new way. They are here at this time, again, to support us in our evolution. Their big message is one of balance."

The session is complete.

Turning to the facilitator, I ask to walk Spirit Walker back to the barn. As I enter the round pen, he walks over and nuzzles at my heart, again. I hold the halter open for him, an invitation to come with me, and he slips his muzzle into it. His victim cloak has been transmuted to a shield of co-empowerment and I see him differently now. He's found a balance between being a horse, a teacher, a mirror, and a wise friend. He's not concerned about expressing his support, affection, or love for another being, especially a man. By example he reminds me to be more expressive, vulnerable, relaxed as a man willing to embrace the energies of the new masculine and feminine. I can feel his heart radiating power, certainty, devotion, and warmth in every step he takes, each step in unison with mine. And in my heart, a heart unlocked by vulnerability, supported by his courage, empowered by the inspiration of possibilities, and now exposed–committed to the doorway and corridor of evolution–I know Spirit Walker journeys beside me, his invitation to be buddies.

I am woman	I am the new masculine
A reflection of the sun	Spirit shining on a new day
Daughter of the earth	Grounding deep within the earth
Truth of life	Offering space for the heart to grow
The balance in the new age	Allowing my wholeness to be in balance
The dance of human evolution	Amongst all humans
The manifestation of those before me	I stand as an inspiration for the coming generation
The holder of my dreams	To hold a new dream of equality
The cycle returning	Shedding the old patterns of domination
The movement to a new energy spin	And creating a new energy to move us together
I am worth it	To stand in a new measure of self-worth as a man.
I am woman	I am the new masculine
The space between the glittering stars	Like the grandfathers of days past I stand behind
Love that holds a community	The creation of a new community
The flow into higher consciousness	Heart open, aligning with nature
Trusting my instincts	In balance with the higher frequencies of life
Heart of consciousness	Respecting all connections and never alone
Teacher to the young	I stand as the new teacher
Expressing a new dream	Creating new symbols for myself and my quest
Embracing opportunities	To cast out the karma of the past
Aligning with the new energies	And witness the coming of a higher vibration
Connected to my Spirit.	To breathe in a new world.

To be read by column top to bottom "I am woman"
then "I am the new masculine"
then read line by line across "I am woman, I am the new masculine".

Andre and his buddy, Spirit Walker

Andre Leclipteux is a FEEL Practitioner and director at Horse Spirit Connections. He is also Shamanic Coach having graduated from the Institute of Shamanic Medicine. He also leads men's group in exploring and defining the masculine in today's world, incorporating native ceremonies with horse wisdom and interaction.

Working with the horses and incorporating Shamanism ignited his new journey, one that allowed him to seek, explore, and define himself and help others do the same. A graduate of the Epona Partners Program at the Eponaquest Center in Arizona, Andre continues to work with horses on the ground helping others achieve self-empowerment and emotional growth.

As a graduate of Sheridan College, Andre has been involved professionally in advertising, marketing, promotions, and communications over the last 25 years. In 1986, he left the agencies to start his own consulting business. As his clients grew, in 1994 he formed Wings & Ink, a successful marketing communications firm with his wife and partner, Wendy Golding. The company grew steadily into a multimillion-dollar corporation and received national as well as international recognition for its creative work.

Andre retired from corporate life in 2010 after the sale of Wings & Ink to an international corporation. "There was a tremendous satisfaction in knowing what you dreamed and birthed had evolved and reached independence." He now devotes his time to the growth of Horse Spirit Connections.

Andre has a passion for horses, sound business acumen, and a desire to see people heal and lead heart-filled lives. Whether in the saddle or on the ground, Andre is quite comfortable connecting to horse energy. Andre invites you to learn more about the transformative work with the horse by visiting www.HorseSpiritConnections.com and he can be reached at Andre@HorseSpiritConnections.com

CHAPTER 7

Emotions, Messages, and Healing Horses

By Beverley Clifton

As a child, I loved all the horses. To me, horses have always been the most magnificent animals on the planet. I remember watching them on the black-and-white television, and I remember my colouring books where I would colour in the horse pictures first. I would read about them in story books. I imagined that my toy hobby horse was real. We would soar over make-believe jumps I made in the small back garden typical of a suburban home in the northwest of England. As I got older my fascination with ponies and horses increased. Every year I would ask Father Christmas for a horse. Every Christmas I would check the garage to see if he had delivered. One year there was a second-hand bike in there with my name on it. It was light blue and silver, on the handle bar was a new bell. I did not receive a horse but instead a bike, definitely a surprise, and this was good. I had my very own two-wheeled bike. I couldn't wait for the rain to stop. I knew where I wanted to go as I had walked to the countryside before. At every opportunity I would venture out on my bicycle; first crossing over the main road at the zebra crossing, and then I would peddle as hard and as fast as I could up the next road and eventually over the humped-back bridge. The houses across the canal were larger and spaced out more. The trees were huge; laurel and hawthorn hedges replaced the brown fences and privet that I knew on the tight-housed street where I lived. And then there came the farm houses, in the distance were clumps of trees and fields. As I raced along the smooth surfaced avenues, the bridle path neared. Breathless, I would feel my thigh muscles burn; just a few more minutes and I'd be on that packed stony path kicking up loose gravel with the speed of my rubber bike tyres. There were fields of burnt sienna, yellow, and sections of green forest on either side of the path. My bike rumbled over a cattle grid and my arms shook, making me feel more filled with excitement. If I were on a horse we would have leapt over the grid, and cleared it with ease, no problem! Slowing down to catch my breath I knew I was seconds away from the destination.

And there they were, horses, all seven of them, two dark bay and four grey grouped together, and a liver chestnut close by. It was usually the lone liver chestnut that looked up from his meal of forage first. I knew they'd all be there, and I would stay for hours just to watch them. I always hoped that one or two of the herd would come to visit me from their field and share themselves for a while. I loved how the horses moved, and the sounds they made. I loved to hear them munching urgently on the grass, as if there would be none left for tomorrow. The nickering sounds they made to each other, and sometimes when they noticed me; "Hello!" I loved the swishing sound their tails made as they warded pesky flies away. And as I watched them meander toward me as I stood at the gate to their fields, I felt accepted. As they came close, I felt giddy with excitement. I always wanted to open the gate into their space, but never dared, fearing the farmer would not like that. I loved to touch them if they came close enough; and to feel their breath, warm from their large nostrils. When they nuzzled, their whiskers would tickle my hand as they searched and hoped for carrot treats. I felt that this acknowledgment was the best gift in the world. I loved to share the treats amongst them and I felt sad when all the treats were gone because that was the time when they would slowly return to graze on the land. I was always careful not to get caught on the barbed wire that divided our worlds. I felt alive with the horses, I loved their distinctive smell, and I loved to watch their movement, sometimes they would be quick and alert, ears forward, necks straight, making them appear larger than ever. Once I saw them in flight, they were moving fast, their muscles taut, their hooves pounding the ground. I was surrounded by their physical and emotional energy. Something must have aroused them. Perhaps it was me cycling up the bridle path? Mostly their motion would denote grace, balance, and sturdiness. They allowed me to watch them play and groom each other. I remember always dreaming of riding one of them, perhaps owning a horse of my own one day. I would be happy to have complete immersion into their world. As a child, I felt gratitude in their wondrous presence. I always felt grounded, calm, and quiet in their presence. They always allowed me to feel alive, to live in the moment. The horses showed me then "there is only one moment and the moment is now."

The Lament

As a young adult I was very busy. Every minute of every day was accounted for. Between my career, committees, university courses, volunteer work, marriage and divorce, my life became a whirlwind of activity, and ultimately very exhausting. I was always in flight. And yet, there always seemed to be an ache, buried within the busyness. I spent a lot of my young adult life listening and participating in conversations with voices, scurrying around in my ever-busy brain. The internal dialogue was often sensible and informative providing me with positive ideas and insights to enable me to make good life choices. Some of the conversations in my head were confrontational, critical and unkind, yet caught my attention anyway. Sometimes in that head space there would be light banter, humour, sarcasm, and reasoning. Then there were the great debates; the "should haves" and the "what ifs?" Not to mention endless "to do" lists.

For many years the din was constant, back and forth, and well rehearsed to the point where I believed in much of the content. I believed that I was not good enough, not prepared, nor intelligent enough during the comparisons I made between myself and others. When I went shopping for clothes for myself I would be riddled with guilt once I got home. Looking back, I think how awful, and how ridiculous, as it was necessary for me to look professional for my career. This particular struggle seems ludicrous now. Worse than this I believed that I did not deserve to be loved. In retrospect, I can hardly believe that I got out of bed in the morning to go to work. The truth to my ability to perform as a professional was an invincible disguise that I wore cloaking my inner self. The mask I showed the world was of happiness and competency. I would move through my daily life and would recall many past memories. In reality, I had looming worries about my future. I became depressed and anxious at the same time. I was also emotionally numb, completely unable to pay attention to the emotions and messages that were being sent to my physical body. I recognize now that during that period I was far too occupied and mentally distraught, to even be aware that previous loss and trauma was actually locked in my body. And my body was screaming for attention.

During the years I had denied myself the opportunity to experience any emotional feelings. The result of suppressed emotions manifested in my body. In every cell and fibre. My immune system became compromised. I caught colds and flu, and anything popular at the time. I began to lose weight. I had a stomach ache every day. Over time the muscles in my neck, upper back, jaw, and other parts of my body began to seize. It wasn't until my jaw completely seized to the point that I could not open my mouth that I decided that something must be wrong.

You see, being continuously distracted with my career, courses, and such, allowed me to avoid the inevitable. That was of course honouring myself, my emotions, and feelings. As dark and depressing this period of my life was, I do believe this experience was necessary in my life. I went through this disturbing, wretched period for many reasons. I had to face the cause of the disconnect of living in my head, and not fully connected as a whole person. I needed to realize that I did have the right, and I deserved to be happy. During my mid teenage years I faced much change and challenge. I had no control over my own life, decisions were made and life as I knew it came to an end. It seemed like one traumatic event led to another. It was finally time for me to acknowledge the reality and affect of these unexpected events. I thought the trauma of these disturbing events would go away and fade in time but the ugliness of it all was buried within. Time heals? In my case not without intervention. I was eventually diagnosed as a textbook case, of an individual dealing with Post Traumatic Stress Syndrome. With the help of medical intervention, treatment, support, and much self exploration, (the hardest work I have ever done); I actually did start to feel better. I will always be grateful for traditional therapy; as I worked through proven practice, processes and procedures I became more self aware and positive in my life. I was able to begin to admit, deal with, and unravel my personal pain, losses, and grieve those earlier years. This dark and painful period did begin to slowly pass into a light of possibilities.

I was tired. Tired of living the fast-paced, incongruent life that I had created. I had nothing to avoid, deny, or run away from anymore. From Gestalt theory, practice, and years of psychotherapy, I knew it was time for me to explore what was truly meaningful for me. While I did feel better most of the time, I believed that there had to be a much deeper and longer lasting level of healing. For me, it was the horses that enabled me to reach that deeper space. Over the last decade I have made emotional connections with people and many horses. Four horses in particular have connected with me and have tried to teach me to be emotionally awake. I am honoured to describe and explain my healing journey and experiences with them.

The Horses and the Healing

The minute I walked into the barn where my friend was taking riding lessons, I knew I had entered a space of endless possibilities with horses. The atmosphere there promised me magic. Magic that had disappeared too soon from my childhood. For the first time in years I felt excited and happy. There was that familiar smell of manure and hay, and a flash of wondrous dreams and memories. There were horses in their stalls munching, nickering. Tack, saddles, bridles, bits, and brushes were visible. I felt an excitement throughout my entire body. I was on sensory overload. I was greeted by the owner of the establishment; her passion and energy were contagious. She led me through the stables and as we turned the corner, there stood an enormous dark horse in the cross ties. He was huge, with white on his face and legs. Truly a splendid horse. We were introduced. His name was Ringo. He was to be my first horse riding lesson in years. I gasped, "Are you for real?" Apparently so. I wasn't sure if what I was feeling was fear or joy, but what I felt in my body was a surge of emotional activity.

I instantly loved Ringo. As I began to learn how to groom him, I was in sheer awe of his size. He stood quietly, and as I brushed and massaged his giant body, I thought I could make a career out of grooming him. Once again I began to appreciate the power and magnificent presence of the horse. Of Ringo. He was warm to the touch, his muzzle was soft, and as he took a breath, his nostrils widened inhaling more oxygen than I could imagine. He breathed slowly and deliberately. His eyes were soft and brown with a sparkle of mischief. I noticed how his withers would twitch every now and then. I remember how my hands and arms ached, and I remember lifting his huge feet to pick out his hooves and shoes. I also remember how attentive and focused I was during this procedure. To be elsewhere meant I might easily be accidently hurt. One of Ringo's favourite expressions was to paw the air; he would alternate each leg, as if to dance, and I would laugh. He would be "that" horse to pull off my hat when my back was turned, only for me to retrieve it from his smiling mouth. What a joyful character to be around! He was such a caring, comical individual, with a huge heart and loving energy.

It was Ringo who taught me as an adult to be alert and to truly enjoy the present. I finally came to understood this concept. He taught me to enjoy the moments as they unfolded. This is the nature of the horse. Ringo taught me to feel joy, "to commune with nature, love and beauty. To laugh, goof and dream." I will be forever grateful to Ringo for this gift. As I spent time learning new skills with Ringo, I also began to gain and feel confidence within myself, and was in awe as this confidence spilled into my daily life. Giddy feelings and emotions erupted when I was with him, almost like a young girl's first crush! I had not truly felt this since my years at high school. Ringo changed my life; he helped me to open my heart, so that I could be true to myself and go forward to address and claim my "dream of a lifetime.". That was when I was 43.

My Next Ride was a Mercedes

The search for a horse of my own began the journey into horse ownership. I had an idea of what my horse should look like, be like, but I had no idea of the entire package I was about to receive. The mare came into my life quite unexpectedly. The first time I saw her she was performing proudly under saddle. Like a finely tuned machine, she was working in rhythm, her body was supple, straight, and was collected with impulsion as she connected with her riding partner. What a vision as she danced around the arena. Within a month I was her new owner. She was an older mare, a "school mistress," a "been there done that" type, everything from schooling, showing, to teaching youngsters how to ride. She had also thrown two foals, first Mozart and later Deborah's Vision. Mercedes above all else was born to nurture. And, would be a "babysitter" for me in my quest to learn to ride.

When Mercedes came home, I was thrilled, excited, and exhilarated for our life together. She on the other hand was matter of fact, confident in herself, and rather aloof. She also arrived with a back hoof wrapped and bandaged with care. She had an abscess. Whatever that was, I was assured it was nothing serious. I could not ride her until the abscess had cleared. I did not know this meant that the healing could take up to two weeks or longer. I learned very quickly that horse ownership included periods of time where one must have knowledge to deal with the anatomy of the horse and their unexpected injuries. I lacked the experience, knowledge, and confidence and questioned "what in the world had I got myself into?"

My first lesson from Mercedes was how to cope with vulnerability. My life, now with my own horse, had changed significantly and I could feel the onset of panic. Mercedes was my dream come true and all I knew was that I had better learn everything I could and fast! I was blessed to have patient, willing, knowledgeable, and experienced horse people around me. They knew I wanted to learn, and they were genuine and willing teachers. I chose to challenge the vulnerable state I was feeling. In the past, being vulnerable cost me my life as I knew it. This is my life now and I had nothing to lose.

I spent days becoming familiar with Mercedes. She was kind, serious, and reserved. She was also a wonderful patient. She would stand quietly and still for ages, holding her own energy as I became familiar with leg wraps, techniques, duct tape, vet wrap, animal lintex, even preemie diapers to cradle her hoof to ensure the medicine wouldn't leak out. Mercedes and I walked many miles during her healing period. Never once did she strike out during the bandage procedure, nor refuse to follow me on yet another walk around the arena. Finally, the time had come for me to try my riding skills with her. My first experiences "riding" her were quite humbling. As I mounted her, I felt so proud, and sat tall as I cued her to move on. Off we went, until it was time to turn into the first part of a serpentine. This involves steering. I wasn't sure why she wasn't going in the direction of my cues. I knew she knew how to circle and change direction. I had witnessed this. I thought I knew the riding aids to give a horse to execute these movements. And so I asked again and again. Nothing. She stopped, I jiggled. This went on for a while and each time I began to feel rather frustrated. Obviously the actions I was taking were not effective. Instead of giving up, or feeling powerless, I asked my coach for help. The lesson I received from feeling frustrated was to lead Mercedes, and ask her to move with more serious intent. I had to change my approach. I needed to believe in what I was asking her to do. Mercedes requested that I needed to keep practicing! This was the beginning of our journey together. Mercedes insisted that I give her the riding aids properly, that I follow her work ethic, or she would not perform! This was for my own good, at the barn, and as I learned later, during my professional life. She was a joy to ride once I had caught on to her ways! Mercedes was a lady, she loved to be groomed and pampered. We spent hours together. Laughing, learning, riding, and chilling. She stood over me when I landed on the ground, and waited patiently for me to climb back into the saddle to continue. As they said she would, she truly did look after me. Mercedes took me over my first jump. She took me to my first horse show. She was worth her weight in gold. She was my first true equine friend, and understood the necessary challenges she gave to me. Mercedes knew all along that what I needed in my life was for me to learn to believe in myself. I felt that she instinctively knew what lessons to present to me to move me along this path. We had been together for four years when I had to make the hardest decision of my life.

Mercedes became sick. She was in pain and lame, and very distressed. After many months of total care and every attempt to enable rehabilitation, the veterinarian could not intervene further medical care. I had to make an alternative decision for her. This was the most difficult experience I have ever had as a horse owner, but especially as a human being. How could I end this beautiful life? How could this be? What will I do without her? She was my dream come true. My Mercedes.

The following time period I experienced a gamut of emotions; I was sad, angry, frustrated, frightened. Grief stricken. I felt tremendous grief, loss, and sadness that I had only once experienced before. Only this time I allowed myself to cry, out loud for hours, and whenever I felt it necessary to release the inner pain and sorrow. I allowed myself to feel my anger and guilt and despair. I also felt the haunting of the uncontrollable loss I had experienced during my teenage years. Mercedes in her death facilitated a safe haven for me to release all the sadness that was left, embodied in my heart. I granted myself permission to feel all the emotional pain of losing my most treasured gift and dream come true.

Mercedes. It was not until recently that I realized I was able to grieve and let go in a healthy way. I came to acknowledge and accept my loss. I truly appreciated her, and became emotionally capable to celebrate her life and our time together. Mercedes gave me many gifts. She is with me always, and is the Spirit I see frozen across the sun on a cold winter's day.

Under Odinn's Watchful Eye

Austin Plays Soccer

Austin Sprite

In a field was a young thoroughbred, wrapped in a quilted blanket waiting for his forever home. Austin horse accidently came into my life. Well, not really, as there isn't any such thing as an accident. Austin came into my life with a purpose. He was turning 3 at the time and very naive. What was I thinking? My equestrian team of friends promised they would help me with him. Thankfully they have remained true to their promise. I thought I knew and had enough equine experience to be effective with a youngster. And so our unassuming journey together began. Austin and I spent many months interacting with each other. Austin made it clear to me that in order for him to learn anything I had to have a definite plan in mind. Every time we were together, I would need to be organized, focused and determined, and definitely armed with treats. The first six months proved to be the biggest learning curve of my life.

For the most part, Austin and I thoroughly enjoyed learning lessons from each other. With Austin horse in hand (attached to a lead rope), and myself implementing ground exercises, Austin taught me how to lunge him in the round pen. If my body was not in the correct position to drive him forward he would stop and turn to face me. He would not move again properly until I had corrected myself in both my mind and body. I absolutely had to be clear with intent and focused on him. Nothing else was to be of importance during our sessions. He taught me to get over my frustrations, and to repeat my requests over and over until we were both attentive and mindful of the lessons being delivered!

He was very curious and very quick to learn. I was usually only one day ahead of him in his training and in my education as a "trainer" as I learned what the next steps were from his real trainer (my coach.) There have not been many other times in my life where I actually felt inept as I did during these early training days with Austin. Once again, I was learning more about myself than I think the horse was learning from me. Austin taught me patience, he taught me to notice, to be more observant, and to consider other methods and combinations of delivering information to him. Only when I executed various possibilities for his learning, did I receive the most favourable outcome, for both of us. Most of all Austin made me laugh and enabled me to genuinely enjoy the feeling of happiness in the moments we shared. Austin returned the joy that had been stolen from me as a young adult. I relearned how to play, and yes, I deserve to play too! (*Play is the highest form of research*—Einstein) Austin demonstrated much desire to learn, to be a "good boy." Joy and satisfaction endured as he allowed me to appreciate and recognize the small steps of improvement in our learning together. He even learned to play "yoga ball soccer," all in the name of carrot treats when he scored a "goal!" He was hilarious.

I have also experienced much success during this relationship, the more successful Austin was as a learner, the more confident I became as his facilitator. This was paramount for me, to gain confidence to continue with the quest of working with a young horse. What a boost this has been in my abilities to communicate, ask and listen, and to therefore carry these skills into my everyday life. However, there were many lessons repeating the same theme. Ground manners. More often than not the greatest test in this curriculum were teaching and maintaining Austin's manners. This horse is a very large, strong, and powerful beast. I am slight in comparison. It was absolutely necessary that Austin be taught to respect my "space." Any swift move from his powerful head, leg, foot, could render me injured or even worse. For my personal safety, I learned the importance of setting my own personal space, and setting my own boundaries and limits with Austin. It is curious how the personal space and boundary lessons with Austin were critical pieces of information for me to practice in my own personal life. One afternoon, I found myself ending a training session very quickly only to drive myself to the local emergency unit. I was leading Austin through a gate when my finger got caught, Austin pulled, the gate won, and my finger was instantly dislocated. It was obvious that medical assistance was necessary. At this particular time in my life, I was experiencing difficulties with my life partner. I was not paying attention to what I was doing with Austin in fastening the gate and I got hurt. This situation paralleled my personal life. The lesson here from my equine friend was for me to "pay more attention." Once at home I started to pay attention. I continue to pay attention.

The time came for Austin to be trained under saddle and allow a rider to sit on his back to learn the cues and aids necessary to become a riding horse. We acquired more skills, trust, and balance. Through the expert tutelage of his trainer, Austin became confident in his work and himself. We have had many riding experiences together, most of them have been very successful, fun, and even exhilarating. Then one time at the end of a quiet evening hack, without any warning, this part of our journey came to an end. I found myself on the hard ground. Austin had panicked and spooked at something. He bucked high, hard, and fast. I had no chance of staying in the saddle. As I landed I knew I was hurt. I had landed on the right side of my neck and shoulder. The wind had been knocked out of me and I could not move, then I felt the pain in my neck. I also felt each part of my body as I asked every limb to move. I was Ok. The fall resulted in a serious case of whiplash. Along with the whiplash my confidence was shattered. I knew at the time of the fall I felt very frightened and was very aware of the physical threat to my body. What I did not realize at the time was the impact on my emotional and mental state. As I recovered I naturally began riding Austin again, but our horse and rider partnership was not the same as it was before. I knew I had to relax. Austin is a very sensitive horse, when he feels that I am in a hurry, anxious, or frustrated he will not comply. Even when I am wearing my "happy mask" Austin sees right through it. He knows when I am not being authentic, as he is able to sense the various degrees of my emotional energy. I have learned that different emotions present different vibrations. Austin is quick to pick up the differences. Austin always mirrors my true feelings, projecting back what I need to see.

Whenever I am frustrated or bring my work day to the barn, he will become agitated especially when I try to groom him. This frustrates me further. Not until I make a conscious effort to either recognize my energy and take some deep breaths to relax, does Austin change his behaviour. You can never lie to a horse, especially Austin. It took me a long time to figure this out; it has also taken me a while to understand why our riding relationship was totally off kilter. I would climb onto Austin's back with confidence galore, only to realize that what I was truly feeling in my body was fear. Of course Austin picked up on my anxiety, and I would feel his anxiety in return surging through my heart and stomach. Proliferating the fear back and forth we had it; "the dance of mistrust." It was not until I acknowledged and admitted to Austin how frightened I felt when I tried to ride him that our relationship began to change back. Fear had given me a choice; *forget everything and run or face everything and rise*. I feel blessed to be able to share my incredible journey with Austin. As I continue to watch him grow up and mature, I feel my heart swell with intense energy and pleasure. I am guessing he feels the same way about my new development in emotional agility.

The Autumn of my Life

Some horses are named appropriately. I have recently met and connected with an Icelandic horse, whose name is Odinn, meaning inspiration. Odinn inspired me to write about my emotional awakening; using the healing help of horses with whom I have previously made a connection. I have sat with Odinn in his field, and I have quietly, purposely silenced myself to hear his messages. Odinn is strong in body, mind and, soul. I would describe Oddin as the guardian of all the horses at his farm. The other horses are separated from him by fences, they are herds within a herd, together as one. And Odinn shares his space with a lovely Icelandic chestnut mare.

Oddin is the first horse to greet the humans at his gate as we drive up the driveway to the barn; he is the last horse we see as he watches and sends us on our way. I leave the barn with his image in my thoughts. He stands a mere 13 hands, he is a sturdy, and dark horse. Odinn possesses the thickest, longest dark mane, tinged with a hint of titian red. His dense forelock shadows his soft eyes; his all seeing, all knowing watchful eye. I am sure Odinn is a very old soul, even though he is only 20. All the other horses on the farm respect him as he respects them all in return. He quietly stands his ground; he is non-judgmental, kind, and trusting.

It seems odd that Odinn and I connected, as I never did have an agenda with Odinn; to ride or train him, yet he was always curious to see me, and stay with me during our visits over the gate even after the carrots were gone. Did he choose me to be his acquaintance or did I choose him?

I know that when I spend time with Odinn I become grounded. His energy is very strong and soothing, he allows me to be part of his presence and makes me breathe, one breath at a time. What is it about this dark horse that continues to draw me into his space?

Odinn's story is that he was taken away from Iceland, his homeland, when he was 8 years old. He travelled to a new country, met new humans, experienced a different climate, and foraged unknown territory, even the food must have tasted different. Trusting that all would be well, young Odinn became faced with adversity. His new owner was rough and harsh. Odinn endured abuse to his young body and good nature for almost five years. Fortunately, Odinn was released from that environment and was delivered to a most caring and loving woman, (she is still with him today). It took his new owner more than two years of consistent ground work; Reiki, energy healing, endless retraining, unconditional love, trust and confidence building. This is our connection, the loss of innocence, identity and familiarity, naivety and parallel experiences. Thankfully various levels of intervention enabled us to recover some of what was lost. I think we can both be described as wounded healers. Today, we are both resilient and strong in character, yet I still know the haunting depth to which emotional trauma can reside.

I see Odinn every day, his lessons, body language, and message to me are always the same, "always know you are strong, believe in your values, all will work out as it is intended." I look down at his furry legs and see that the hair there is growing thick and long, in time for the winter and it is only August. As a further reflection of Odinn's knowledge, I must remind myself daily to accept myself as the person I have become. Odinn has brought back memories of a time where I sincerely felt accepted and valued. In my current life I am happy and appreciate where this is true again. How fortunate am I to have an alliance with a "dark horse." Since Odinn has been in my life when I have experienced strange dreams, I have chosen to pay attention to their meaning. I have dreamt of the horse ancestors, and I now accept and understand how their wisdom helped me through my acquaintance with Ringo, Mercedes, Austin, and Odinn.

The Harvest

As an educator myself, I truly believe in lifelong learning. I continue to study and love the challenge of a new endeavour. As I was searching the internet one day, I came across the most interesting site: Horse Spirit Connections. I knew I had to go there, and pursue this opportunity.

It was a dreary day in March when I drove onto the property of Horse Spirit Connections, I felt an energy shift; the winter-bare trees hung over the lane way with a greeting that made me feel safe and peaceful. As I walked into the lodge, I recall the vibrant colours and the beautiful art, hanging on the walls, books, feathers, and a distant scent that was unrecognizable to me filled my senses. I remember the warm reception I received, the tour to the barn, meeting the horse teachers, and the resonance I felt there. I remember being welcomed by one horse in particular. She was tucked cosily in a far stall and she came to greet me, with her head over the door she actually touched my shoulder with the side of her face. We walked back to the lodge and at this point the words I was hearing echoed many of my thoughts and feelings. This was a sacred place and I knew that I would return. I knew I had to return, but to do so I realized that I was taking a leap of faith. I had to find money to pay for the program; I needed to receive permission to take a leave of absence from my work, organize and prepare lessons; at home: the food, bills, laundry, pet duty, and gardening needed to be tended to.... As many women know, juggling a full-time career, with home and family can be chaotic at the best of times! What I thought would become obstacles, were actually non-issues. The money and time I required came to fruition effortlessly, as though they were gifted to me; most important I had love and support from my family. The following May I began the most empowering journey as a FEEL student. I had no idea how much I had to learn.

To rediscover the journey that began for me as a child has empowered me to live an authentic life. I am able to take emotional risks. In the FEEL practice, emotions serve as the cornerstone for information. In my experience, emotions are messages that transmit energy through the physical body to highlight information necessary for us to be fully aware of what we are actually feeling. Throughout my childhood I was acutely aware of how I was feeling and where exactly in my body I was feeling the emotion. Growing up in a culture that denied feelings and discouraged displays of emotion, I learned to suppress sadness and tears, anger, frustration, and exhilaration. And so by the time I was a young adult I had mastered the art of being emotionally incongruent. What I presented to the world was not how I was feeling. I have learned that horses are highly tuned to the various vibrations emotions emit. Forty-five years have passed since my first experiences with horses. I realized during the time I was a FEEL student that I was able to reawaken my emotions that were once very clear to me during my early years. As a FEEL student and subsequent practitioner I am now equipped with self-awareness and emotional agility. My emotional awakening and support from the horses has prepared me to further develop my empathetic skills. The horses welcomed me once again and enabled me to understand the importance of being aware, being present, and the importance of being authentic.

This journey has been a privilege and I cannot begin to thank the many horses and people that have helped me along the way. On this path, I intend to share my passion for the horses by marrying my teaching skills, my life's work, to enable people to embrace a more authentic life. I have spent the majority of my adult life teaching young woman and men the importance of being self-sufficient. I have had tremendous opportunities to help shape young lives and intend to continue this route with the help of the horses. At this point know I am "green" to this work and my FEEL practice, but it is time for me to "pay it forward," to help others realize there are new levels and new ways of feeling and healing. Whilst working with the horses I have witnessed "ah-ha moments" and experienced positive changes in other people. People who thought they were stuck somewhere in their lives have been nudged in the right direction. As sentient beings the horses are present to help us, but only when we ask and when we are ready to listen. With the help and wisdom of my equine friends, I want to work with people to help them overcome their doubts, misgivings, and disappointments. These as I discovered are more often than not self-imposed. I know my journey does not end here, once a person embarks on a journey with horses in this way, the journey is for life.

Beverley Clifton

Beverley Clifton has always had a fascination and heartfelt bond with horses. This love began as a young child. During the decade starting in 2004, experiences and opportunities with horses have allowed Beverley to enjoy emotional and spiritual awakening that has called her to work with horses as teachers and healers. Beverley is combining her lifelong work as an educator with the horses and their wisdom to benefit others, so that they too may make and have the courage to change their lives for the better.

Even before her years as a member of the Ontario College of Teachers, Beverley has always been a believer and advocate of *lifelong learning*. She began an apprenticeship in hairstyling in her teens. She became skilled in the trade and proved herself as a hairstylist and successful business owner. After nine years of operating her own salon, Beverley yearned to share and teach her trade and experience with young people. Beverley connected well with her students and has continued to aspire and lead young women and men to become the best that they can be. Beverley has developed a safe and humanistic approach to teaching and delivering curriculum; and as an educator, thousands of students have learned and gained lifelong skills enabling them to become self sufficient contributors to society. Throughout her career in education, Beverley has received awards and recognition, and has continued her studies with the University of Waterloo, Brock University, and is currently completing the Equine Science program through the University of Guelph. Beverley is a recent Graduate of the FEEL program at Horse Spirit Connections in Ontario.

Beverley is looking forward to working and helping people by blending her teaching, creativity, life experiences, and skills in her FEEL practice: *Learning with Horses (the answers are within you.)* Beverley and her lifelong partner now reside in a rural home in Puslinch, Ontario, surrounded by horses, and can be contacted at: learningwithhorses2013@gmail.com

CHAPTER 8
Power of Emotion
By Raymonde Violette

Emotions, according to the Psychology Dictionary, "is a complex psychological state that involves three distinct components: *a subjective experience, a physiological response, and a behavioural or expressive response.*" (Hockenbury & Hockenbury, 2007). Experts believe that there are a number of basic universal emotions that are experienced by people all over the world. They also believe that the experience of emotions can be highly subjective (based on feelings or opinions rather than facts). While we might have broad labels for certain emotions such as angry, sad, or happy, our own unique experience of these emotions is probably much more multidimensional.

As a little girl, I was influenced by the opinions and judgment of surrounding family members and society in general. I would observe, listen, and assimilate their teaching to what was wrong or acceptable. I witnessed how the adults were handling their own emotions. I remember thinking I will never do that as the feeling I had was unpleasant, so I kept quiet and tried to please everybody and carefully avoided disturbing the adults in my surroundings. Occasionally a little voice inside would surface, wanting to see, explore, and venture but I was afraid of rejection, judgment, and shame.

Today, at 67 years old, I realize I had already started to ignore my own emotions during my childhood. To all readers I would like to share with you my first venture. Raised within the Roman Catholic religion, during my teenage years I was captivated by the Catholic Nuns' way of life. In my community they were revered. Ah! This time it was a good feeling, I wasn't afraid. My first adventure would be approved by the people in my community. Now, I would experience the Catholic Nuns' way of living behind closed doors. I was excited; I actually would be living an adventure. After graduation I enrolled to the novitiate with the sisters of Notre Dame du Sacré Coeur, one of the ministries of our province. Nine months later, even though the experience was beneficial, I opted to spend my life helping people as a civilian. I undertook a three-year program in nursing and obtained my license as a registered nurse. Helping people was gratifying and soothing, my life revolved around helping other people; I became addicted if there is such an addiction.... I became an expert in listening to other people's emotions thus refusing to acknowledge my own, additionally I have to mention, growing up with two brothers, releasing tears wasn't an option. The perfect recipe for a super woman.

Additionally, if you ever felt your stomach lurch from anxiety or your heart palpate with fear, then you realize that emotions also can cause strong physiological reactions. Sweating palms, racing heart beat, or rapid breathing are controlled by the sympathetic nervous system, a branch of the autonomic nervous system. It is charged with controlling the body's fight-or-flight reactions. How do we actually express our emotions? I have spent a significant amount of time in my own life interpreting the emotional expressions of people around me. Through my work as a registered nurse and massage therapist, and my journey within the last few years with horses and the FEEL program, I understand that these expressions are what psychologists call emotional intelligence (ability to perceive, control, and evaluate emotions) and these expressions play a major part in our overall body language. Through the FEEL program I have come to understand what is emotional intelligence. It is the ability to get the message behind the emotion, what information is my body trying to convey. Consider anger. What is it that makes me angry? What do I need to do to alleviate and control this emotion. What does it take to correct the situation and then take action? Staying in the moment and true to myself, I am able to cry, feel the emotion, accept, and let go of the emotion and feel my body return to balance.

Horses are prey animals and in order to survive, they have to be sensitive to emotional energy and the intention behind it. Take for example the story of the lion. Horses will often graze unconcerned as a lion who has just eaten a big meal walks right through their pasture. When that same predator is looking for supper, the herd will scatter from a sizeable distance. They have a highly developed ability to respond to subtle changes in stance, muscle tension, breathing, and the general arousal level of other horses and predators and they transfer the ability to people. As prey animals, horses are very tuned into their environment and emotional information is a very large part of their awareness. Although I was aware of the beauty of these magnificent animals and the peace I felt being in the 'horses' presence over the years, what I really came to understand is how powerful they are in facilitating us through our emotions which I will explain to you in my journey as I became certified as a FEEL Practitioner.

Although I was aware and I was pretty good at getting a better handle on my emotions, I was put through the test over the past three years. It was the most difficult time of my life. I am so grateful through my work and journey with the horses with the FEEL program. I would hope so profoundly it became my life path, my purpose, my mission to help others. The emotions felt following the accidental event of my youngest daughter breaking her leg while jumping off a bucking horse and the death of my spouse, unveiled in acute upper back pain. Undoubtedly, I was caught in the vicious cycle of denial, suppressing my emotions. But imagination had me believe that the pain was from physical exhaustion only. Through my work and my journey with horses and the FEEL program, I was able to heal emotionally and physically.

My first love for horses came when I was 6 years old. Every spring my parents would get in the car with my brothers and me and drive to my grandparents. We all got on the sleigh which was hauled by two big draft horses and go to the sugar camp. Next to his agricultural land, located in St André in the northwestern part of New Brunswick, my grandfather owned a maple tree orchard where each spring he would collect the sap from the trees and boil it in a big cauldron over a fire near the camp. The process would take hours before the sap turned into maple syrup. During this time I would play in the snow with my cousins, adults gathered around the fire and in the camp, talking and laughing. It was a family reunion where everybody was happy to share stories after a long cold winter. That year as a brave little 6-year-old I had no fear and walked up to these two big draft horses that towered above me, who stood patiently for their return home. As a child I was in touch with my emotions. I did not feel fear when adults might have been afraid for a child to be that close to such large animal. I remember the softness of their skin, their relaxed body, how they would bend down their head so I could reach them, the breath that would cover my face and unconsciously breathing it in, the smell, how they made me feel as a whole, how they made everything disappear around me feeling that we were in the same bubble. It was magic.

Growing up I eventually lost contact with horses. After graduating from high school, I enrolled in a nursing program. Three years later I successfully became a licensed registered nurse with my home province of New Brunswick. Nursing became my life. During the evening shift while making the medication round at bedtime, I would always carry a bottle of lotion and offer a few minutes of back rub to my patients even though other nurses wouldn't. I could feel the patient relaxing under my hand at the touch of their skin. This was a very important time for me as it gave me a chance to reach out and accompany my patients into their suffering be it physically or mentally. The next day they would report having a good night's sleep. Unbeknownst to me this would be the precursor to a future in massage therapy, energy healing and working with horses. I intuitively knew through the body connection, and the energy healing I was giving to them, by giving them a back massage, I was assisting their traditional medical treatments. During the course of my nursing career I expanded my experience on post-surgical and medicine ward, operation room, emergency room, and became an evening supervisor in a 65-bed hospital.

A few years after graduation, I met the love of my life, Jacques. Our love gave us two beautiful girls, whom I love and cherish. As they were growing, Jacques and I would take them horseback and wagon riding. I remember feeling quietness, time coming to a stop, noticing nature, forgetting the daily busy activities of the day, a well-being in the presence of these magnificent animals. Louise, our youngest daughter, as a child would often play horse. Her bicycle would become her horse, in the house she would imitate their movement and sound, outside while playing with her friends, quite often the games would involve an imaginary horse. Just before her teenage years, Louise started to ask for a real horse, but due to limited space around the house her dream wasn't fulfilled but unconsciously kept in her heart.

After graduation from senior high, Louise under took her studies in mental health at Cité Collègiale in Ottawa. After her graduation she worked as a mental health intervener in her home town. Her clients consisted of patients with schizophrenia, depression, etc. After a few years, Louise realized the frustration in reaching heavily medicated clients. She sought for nontraditional modalities in helping people with mental illness or disorders. By this time she had met her future mother-in-law who was a massage therapist. Collecting all the information and a choice of school, Louise asked me if I would be interested in attending the same program. I knew I was only a few years from retirement and opted to return to school with my own daughter. Over a period of five years, attending part-time courses during the weekends, we both successfully acquired five different modalities for a total of 2,200 hours, and we were both licensed in our own province and successful in building our business. Our preferred technique was undoubtedly polarity. Dr. Randolph Stone, D.O.,D.C.,D.N., created polarity therapy as a synthesis of western medicine and eastern wisdom traditions. In his 50 years of general medical practice in Chicago, he developed a deep understanding of the subtle principles underlying wellness and disease. It is a healing science based on living energy fields which acknowledges and includes all dimensions of a human being; physical, mental, emotional and spiritual. It's a way of working with the fundamental energies of life, a way of bringing these energies into a state of balance and free flow throughout the entire human energy field.

After a few years working with clients as massage therapists, the love of horses was still present in our hearts. What if we could use the presence of the horses in therapy? Does it exist; how and where could we find it? Her eyes lit up at the thought of it. During the winter of 2011, Louise would seek the internet, read all the information she could find regarding horses, their temperaments, characters, horsenality, looked in the for sale sections, online courses, and videos. She would find time to collect everything on horses. It is also when she found Horse Spirit Connections located in Tottenham, Ontario; a not-for-profit corporation dedicated to promoting transformation and personal growth through the wisdom of the horse. We were ecstatic, yes there was such a place in Canada, a place where they offer workshops, where they provide opportunities for individuals to expand their capacity for self-awareness while strengthening their ability to interact successfully with others, engaging participants on physical, mental, and emotional levels all in the company of horses. In June of that same year we attended the Horse Medicine workshop, the focus being on Spiritual growth grounded through the wisdom of the horse. It teaches us how to ride into new directions, to awaken and discover our freedom and power. For myself it was an awakening to emotions pushed away that were just waiting to re-surface and be dealt with, of old beliefs and patterns that kept me from feeling the true self. For the first time, for as long I could remember, I actually got in touch with myself. Who am I? While on site at Horse Spirit Connection, we inquired about the FEEL (Facilitated Equine Experiential Learning) Certification program, a leading-edge modality for developing human potential. Participants learn to create a horse-centered, experiential learning environment that supports personal growth. This was exactly what we were looking for; Louise with her background in mental health, me with my nursing career and both licensed massage therapists, this program would complement and take us to the next frontier in human evolution involving therapy with the horses as facilitators.

By the end of the summer, my daughter and I had found a 5-year-old mare for sale on the Internet. We viewed her information on the web many times, trusting our intuition, and after a long discussion we decided that she was meant for us, she would be our first horse with FEEL program. After travelling two long days, she arrived on October 8th on a Sunday at sundown. Family members and friends gathered to welcome her and have their first peek as she walked out of the trailer. She was a beautiful dark chocolate Rocky Mountain. Standing at 14.3 hands she appeared delicate, feminine, and reserved. Her eyes reflected the joy of getting off the trailer but at the same time uncertainty of where she was and who were all these people surrounding her. Taken to her new rented stall, she stood close to the back, appearing to clutch to the wall. Then came the time for family and friends for meeting and greeting, the in and out of the stall, touching, and tapping. Her eyes wide open, one could feel the uneasiness of all the attention. The next day she received her new name, Allie.

For the next four weeks, my daughter Louise and I with my granddaughter would attend to Allie twice a day. We spent time feeding, cleaning her stall, brushing, lifting her feet, lunging, and walking her. Allie would mill around when we touched her, and she was hard to catch in the field. Being fairly new to horses we all felt nervous around her. We inquired about Allie with her previous owner, she answered that Allie was not used to getting all this loving and kissing attention. Yet, she was so precious to us. Once while free lunging her she brought her head down, licking and chewing. I brought her to a stop, we both breathed in and out, made a heart connection, and I asked if she would be my horse spirit guide. Allie walked straight up to me and put her nose in my hands. My heart was filled with love, compassion, and gratitude.

For more than a year now, Louise, my granddaughter and I had been attending riding lessons twice a week. We made arrangements with our coach to take Allie along with us. On that Saturday morning, feeling very excited, we hooked up the trailer and got the saddle in, then came Allie. With a lot of convincing and half an hour later, Allie got in the trailer. One week later it was time again for another riding lesson. Slowly and gently we had her walk around the trailer, sniff the outside, explained the event of the day then brought her to the back door. After an hour and a half, Allie was just not getting in the trailer this time. By then we were very frustrated and needless to say so was Allie. We then decided to saddle her and brought her in the round pen for a little riding practise. After a short while we both agreed to ride her in the field. On opening the door, she walked out slowly but it was soon after she started to a faster pace and then started to buck. In a moment of panic my daughter decided to jump off, landing on her two feet but soon crumbled to the ground unable to get up, the pain in her right leg was excruciating. About an hour later we were told the bad news, Louise had broken her right leg above the ankle. According to the x-ray, both the tibia and fibula were badly broken. For the next six months, my daughter Louise would be restrained to a wheelchair, a walker, and the cane before starting to walk on her own. I was devastated not only as a mother to see her in such pain but as a healer to see my daughter suffering and possibly not be able to walk normally again. I felt as if the whole world had fallen on my shoulders.

The next day, I drove down to where Allie was kept, to take her out for the day. Now there was just Allie and me. I was very nervous to approach Allie. Standing at a short distance from her, watching her calmly eating her hay, totally relaxed from the frustrating situation she had experienced the day before. How could she be like that? I was crying in despair as to why this had to happen. Why did she have to do that, putting the blame on her. My heart was so much in pain and I was afraid. Finally after a while, I gathered my courage to walk to her and lightly touch her on the shoulder to wish her a good day.

For the next few months, my level of fear was slowly coming down. Quite often my grand daughter and I would attend to Allie after school to settle Allie for the night. We would brush her, comb her mane, clean her feet, touch her and Allie was responding in a positive way. Confidence and trust was settling in. It became more pleasurable to be in each other's company. I learned by respecting her space I gained respect from her. In the course of the next four months, taking her out and feeding her hay in the morning became a ritual. While eating her hay we would breathe together, stand close together almost nose to nose, and feel the energetic flow of our presence in the moment. It was magic. Her odour, her presence, and her whole being made me stronger.

Raymonde's daughter Louise, with Allie

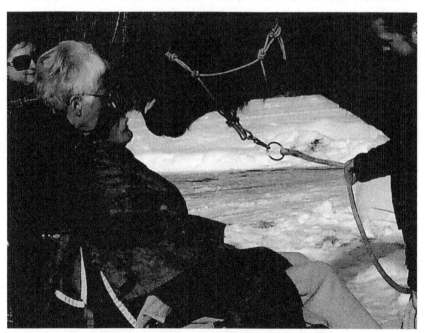

Raymonde and her husband receiving love from Allie

Raymonde and Allie

During the holidays, my husband had fallen twice on the ice. The second time he had really hurt the right side of his back. A month passed, the pain in his back went away, but the limp remained. He visited his family doctor three times during the course of the next three months but was advised that the pain would go away; it was due to his fall. By mid April Louise's leg had healed enough for her to start walking on her own. She put the cane away and sunshine came back in my heart. Even though she was still limping things were looking up. Her interest with horses remained strong.

By the end of April, my husband had to hold on to the walls and furniture to walk as otherwise he would lose balance and fall. I had to believe there was more to it than just the fall on the ice. The six months of stress and worrying for my daughter had taken its toll. By the end of April my husband picked up the cane. Revisiting the doctor, her diagnostic was that he had a stroke. Curiously the rest of his body seemed unharmed. We asked to be referred to a neurologist. Tests were done and he came up with two possible diseases. One of them was ALS (Amyotrophic lateral sclerosis). More tests were done, but he still couldn't pinpoint what was the cause of his limp in the right foot. Revisiting the family doctor we asked to be referred to another neurologist for a second opinion. In June of 2012 my husband was given the diagnostic of ALS. He had just received his death sentence. We were both devastated. Once more the world came crashing down on my shoulders. This time I didn't know if I could bear the pain. My husband of 41 years was going to die. There is no cause or solution for this disease; it was a matter of time. By the end of July that same year he was in a wheelchair. Obviously I made the decision to close my business of massage therapy in order to take care of my husband. I vowed to myself I would give him the best I could, nothing else was important. Even attending to Allie was wiped out of my mind.

By the end of September, I had arranged for my husband to visit Allie at the farm. He was happy; he had developed an affinity with her. At the time Louise and I were both attending the FEEL (Facilitated Equine Experiential Learning) program at Horse Spirit Connection with Wendy Golding and Andre Leclipteux in Tottenham, Ontario. It was an opportunity to practice horse activities we had learned. It would be the Heart Breath activity. I wheeled my husband inside the round pen and Louise as co-facilitator brought Allie to join us inside. Facing Allie I explained and asked Jacques to breathe in and out and when he felt ready to make a heart connection with Allie. Almost immediately, Allie walked up to him, started by sniffing his feet way up to his knees. She then lifted her right foot and slowly tried to stroke his right leg from the knee down. Louise backed up Allie as we didn't want it to be painful for him. He had feeling in his leg but no muscle control of movement. Allie tried again to stroke his leg, Louise backed her off. She nosed him starting at the base chakra way up to the top of his head and came back to his heart. Closing her eyes, her breath was slow and soft as if giving him comfort. I invited my husband to do the same. I could see him relaxing and engulfed in the moment. Once they were complete, I invited Jacques to share his heart's desire. Sobbing he replied, "I asked to be healed." I held him in my arms and we both cried with Allie standing in front of us. I could feel her support and holding a sacred space for us. We drove home in silence. There was a feeling of quietness, time came to a halt, we both felt gratitude for the moments spent with Allie. The turmoil in our hearts had calmed down.

In January 2013, my husband's condition was deteriorating requiring more one-on-one care. Mental and physical fatigue were taking its toll. At night, back pain would wake me up. I felt angry at the world, and I purposely stayed away from seeing people. As my husband was taking a rest after lunch every day, I arranged to have somebody look over him for a few hours during which I could drive and attend to Allie, four to five times a week. This would be a time I would be by myself to unwind. I would be cleaning the stall, giving hay, brushing her. I soon realized breathing in the smell of horse manure, horses' odour, touching her body, interchanging breath, just standing close, and watching her eat would calm my mind. Through a heart connection, I could share the pain in my heart. Feeling the ground under my feet connected me with my body. I felt energized and was able to return home and maintain support for my husband. Attending to Allie became a necessity if I was going to survive these troubled times.

In the last three months of his life, his condition had deteriorated to the point of having great difficulty in swallowing, accumulation of secretions in his throat, loss of appetite, difficulty with speech. Hospitals and nursing homes were not an option as he needed one-on-one around-the-clock care. Qualified people were hired to cover the night and day shift. Between 5 and 10 o'clock p.m. was the only time we were alone in the house. Otherwise people and home care nurses were in and out. Privacy and integrity were lost. Frustration came over me. He wanted to die at home and I also wanted him home to be amongst his family members. On May 27, 2013, my husband passed away. Now I had to face the world without him. Even though I knew all possibilities were out there, I still feared the unknown. Without knowing I had dissociated from the world, I could hear people talking to me but I wasn't listening, didn't retain information, and didn't want to know. I had enough of bad news. Between my daughter's tragic leg injury with Allie and the loss of my husband, I was in survival mode. My life was on hold the past three years. Of course people did not understand the suffering and physical stress this had on me. I created conflicts with other people, but I was trying to protect myself.

In June of 2014, I attended the FEEL Alumni Conference at Horse Spirit Connection in Tottenham, Ontario. On our first day, while attending a seminar in the afternoon, pain in my upper back and shoulders became very uncomfortable. Stretching and changing position hardly relieved the pain. Listening and concentration was practically impossible. I knew it was time for me to get help as I felt I couldn't continue to ignore the pain. My body was calling out for help. Later that afternoon I asked Wendy for a session with one of her horses and explained my situation. This is when she advised that she would demonstrate a new technique called Guided Table Top Healing the next day, and I could be the client on the table.

At first I didn't feel comfortable doing the exercise in front of the group. I felt as if my whole body was going to explode. Would I be able to stay true to myself, would I be hiding or distorting my feelings. I felt like an open book, kind of what you see is what you get, naked, no secrets. What would they think?

It was understood that I would give her an answer by the next morning so I could sleep on it. The next day my decision was made. I hardly had any choices. My body was screaming for help. I gathered all my courage and advised Wendy that I would take her offer and be the client.

I laid down on my back on the table with Wendy as the human facilitator, once the frontal chakras were done she asked that I turn on my stomach and cover the back chakras. Thor, a member of her herd was brought in; he would be the facilitator for the demonstration. Thor approached the table and started to breathe in my right ear. I was encouraged to follow his breath and in the moment I felt discomfort, light pressure, and release inside both ears. How did Thor know I had blocked my ears because I feared receiving any more bad news? He then positioned himself with his rear end aligned with the top of my head; I could feel his energy. With each chakra, I felt release and even physical discomfort.

You see I'm very familiar with the chakras from my years as a nurse and traditional healing and my experience as a massage therapist in the alternative health field. I became very attuned to the body energy system including chakras.

The seven major chakras are powerful energy centers within the body. Chakra means wheels, a vortex of vibration, light, and energy. Some people think of them as little computers, each center processes different information.

First chakra is located at the base of the spine. Out of balance the person might feel unfocused, anxious. With Thor I felt a release, the energy moving and opening.

Second chakra called sacral is located between the lower abdomen and the navel, it contains mental and emotional issues (blame, controlling patterns, emotional feelings example: joy, anger, fear, etc). I felt pressure in my low abdomen and lower back pain.

Third chakra called solar plexus is located one inch below where the ribs meet. It is about self esteem, a place where we feel anxiety, the ego self. It contains much repressed material. Releasing and opening I could feel the energy rotating again and felt sick to my stomach for a moment.

Fourth chakra called heart chakra is about compassion, service, and vocation. Blocks in this chakra will affect the upper back, arms, heart, and lungs. Grief, pain, and anger can live here. When unbalanced, we may feel detached from the world around us. On clearing this chakra lying on my stomach it felt like I had a tight strap around my rib cage. It was difficult to take a deep breath and painful all around my rib cage. I could feel Thor's energy unblocking, opening the space like a funnel, tingling, and warmth. It spoke to me, I had lost control of my life.

Fifth chakra called throat chakra is associated with communication, expression, freedom, responsibility, and leadership. When blocked we feel unable to communicate verbally, physically, and emotionally. Nervousness, anxiety, and fear will reside here. I felt constriction, tightness.

Sixth chakra called third-eye chakra located between and just above the physical eyes. Blocked it may bring eye problems and hearing difficulties. While clearing I felt pain in the inner corner of my right eye.

Seventh chakra called crown chakra located at the crown of the head. When unbalanced it may manifest depression, mentally disconnected, confusion. I felt a painful circle around the crown chakra radiating to my neck and to the top of my shoulders and at the same time warmth and tingling in my shoulder blades. It felt as if it had reopened the connection between my head and back.

Wendy encouraged and suggested that I take time to feel any emotion that was trying to surface. Feeling the sensation at my solar and heart chakra, guilt took over, and I burst out crying. It was painful, yet comforting. I knew we both loved each other very much. I forgave myself for any pain I may have caused him.

Afterward Wendy asked for me to turn on my back. Thor walked over and stood sideways to the table on my right. With my eyes closed I could see energy waves flowing from his guts, above and across my body. It was incredible. I was feeling very relaxed and light. It is amazing how horses engage and work with remarkable speed and facility. I felt releasing of blocked energy on the spur of the moment; it was instant. It was the most profound experience, feeling the release and the energy going to the core of my cells. Horses do not come in with preconceived ideas of who or what this is, or how this person should be in the world, they have no judgment, no filters. When I stood up from the table I felt warmth in my back and could feel the energy circulating. My heart's desire was authenticity towards humanity, and I vowed to be true to myself. My body was light and warm, I felt like dancing.

To my late husband Jacques thank you for your love, your encouragement, and support through all my endeavours. To my beautiful daughters I dedicate this chapter to you. I will always be grateful to you Allie and Thor. You will be forever in my heart. Wendy you not only have helped me on my healing journey you have shown me how I can work with people and horses as a career fulfilling my life purpose of working with this healing modality and incorporating my love of horses.

Looking back on the past three years I have had bitter sweet moments throughout finding my way back to horses yet seeing my daughter have an accident. I now find myself fulfilling the dream my husband and I had in our retirement, to build a house on acreage near my daughter, Allie, and her family. Although Jacques is no longer here with me in body, he is in spirit. My daughter and I have fulfilled our dream and we now have our LERAS Horse Path organisation and have both become FEEL Certified Practitioners. We have our own facility on an exquisite 110 acres surrounded by the serene comfort of nature. The horses are 300 steps from my door step. I am living with the horses, I'm being in their energy, and I am able to practice what I believe in.

Our vision for the future includes the expansion of the herd from four to six horses and to renovate older cabins located in the middle of the land so people can book a weekend, be close to the healing energy of the horses, receive private sessions, or attend workshops. LERAS Horse Path has built a new barn which comprises a meeting room and accommodation for the people to stay overnight. We are so grateful that we are able to incorporate all the different modalities of the FEEL program for people of all ages.

The horses saved my life. They have helped me heal through the most emotional time that I have ever experienced and now even through the pain of the loss of my husband and the pain of my daughter's serious injury I can see a bright future. I am grateful to the horses for helping me through this. Some friends and acquaintances would ask why are you moving way out to the country, you will be far from the hospital and the stores, why are you working with these horses? That is hard work for a woman. I would respond, I love being in nature, I love working with the horses, I have a purpose, I am happy, I'm able to combine my traditional medical background as a nurse and my alternative healing work that I do with massage therapy clients. I incorporate that with the profound healing therapy work with horses that take the people to such a deeper level of healing, connecting on an emotional level.

I'm so grateful and blessed as every day is a new adventure.

I hope that my story is an aspiration to all of those that even in the darkest hour, the light of the sun will shine again.

Silent Powers in My Life

Intuition and knowledge give me the tools
To discern the right moment
To bring forth life's creation

I may fall, I may hurt
But keeping balance
Keeps me standing

I felt rejected by mother's love
But remembering her protection under her umbrella
Turned my belief into forgiveness

Standing alone in the face of power
Shook my foundation
Perseverance made me stronger

From my womb, the birth of my children
Gave me strength against all odds
Only fear tried to destroy

Death of a love one
Took me down to a road of thorns
Nature showed me the beauty of death

Who am I
Only the present will inform
As the source and distant ray of light may distort

I may think I am well surrounded in comfort
Only when I am forced to disrobe
I see my soul

Through the blue flame of fire, I see myself
Through the orange, I see an angel
Through the red, I saw the support of humanity

Confronted by personality ailments
Unstable situation
Authenticity kept me true

Raymonde Violette

Raymonde Violette

Raymonde Violette first discovered her love of horses at the age of 6. In the springtime during maple sugar season, she would go with her family to her grandparent's farm, where they would all get into a sleigh hauled by a team of draft horses and ride to the maple sugar camp. It was magic. Not having forgotten this love of horses, as a young mother, Raymonde would often take her two young daughters for horseback and wagon rides.

After graduating from high school, Raymonde started her career as a registered nurse. She loved helping people get through illness, nursing became her life. As an inquisitive person and dedicated to her patients healing, she took on many responsibilities in her nursing career.

Retiring in 2006, she undertook her studies in massage therapy. She became a successful certified massage therapist in her home province of New Brunswick, offering a variety of well mastered treatments such as; Swedish massage, polarity, hot stone therapy, Raindrop™ and specific massage techniques for people undergoing cancer treatment and accompanying the dying. After embarking in this new career, Raymonde found a new spark in her heart as she assisted clients in their struggles, be they physical, mental, or emotional.

As a former practicing registered nurse and massage therapist, Raymonde decided it was time for her to walk the talk. In 2009 she rediscovered her love for horses and the human/horse relationship in which the horse is the teacher. She furthered her studies and became a Certified Practitioner of the FEEL (Facilitative Equine Experiential Learning) program at Horse Spirit Connections in Tottenham, Ontario.

Raymonde invites you to come and discover your authenticity and the way to a new level of conscious living through the way of horses. Find more information about Raymonde and her program at www.lerashorsepath.com and Facebook/Learning the Path of the Horse.

CHAPTER 9

Sunny with a Chance of Tornado

By Jennifer Garland

This is a story about transformation. It's a story about a horse named Sunny who together with other horses shared their wisdom along a trail of life experiences. It's about how I learned to embrace success on my own terms in spite of the storms that hit my life.

What is success? How do you measure it? Is it about making it to the top of the corporate ladder? Is it about personal achievements and community involvement? Is it a balance of both? Why is being "successful" even important to me? Why is being successful important to any of us?

I have always been a bit fixated on being a "successful" person. Who knew that a particular horse or horses could teach me about this elusive goal? But I have become a better leader, taking each moment, each day as it comes thanks to an unlikely herd of horses as my guides. They've given me reason to pause and take note of the way I move in this world and the impact I have on others. Most importantly, they've made me appreciate the many dimensions of success, while learning to live life fully with intent.

I met my first horse as a kid. We lived in a new subdivision in a rural community. A boy down the road had a paint pony. Back and forth across the fields, we rode that pony for hours. My heart raced along with us. Away from a house defined by rules and expectations, I was filled with a sense of unbridled freedom as we rode with abandon. We were too young to know the risks involved and too young to care. Then the boy moved away, taking his pony with him. I pined to have my own horse. The following Christmas, Santa left a horse for my Barbie doll–a golden palomino.

I lived for some time without horses until a friend in high school invited me to a horse camp. That week the horses took us swimming and cantered without worry, running up and down the surrounding hills. While I didn't have a connection with any particular horse, I did develop a crush on one of the ranch hands. I wanted to ride off into the sunset with my cowboy.

Instead off to college and university I went, experiencing the high of academic achievement. Life got serious and full of expectation when I landed my first job. In my twenties, I was fixated on being a "career girl." My first purchase was a corporate blue suit. A high achiever with an insatiable hunger to succeed, my life was all about work. Seeking approval and acceptance from others as a measure of my triumphs, I wanted to make an impression. Fear of failure caused me much anxiety. I had yet to learn that the greatest wisdom comes from our mistakes. Depending on the situation or a particular trigger, my anxiety would manifest itself into a burst of uncontrollable tears as I spun out of control in a whirlpool of emotion. I didn't know how to channel my anger or frustration. Confrontation and conflict placed me out of my comfort zone. My inner samurai warrior was just waking up, getting ready to fight. With the outside world, I shared a sunny disposition, but within me there was a stormy undercurrent with a chance of tornado.

By my early thirties, my quest for success had manifested into a big title, a number of professional awards, a folder full of fan mail, a good income, two young daughters, a husband, and a chocolate lab named Monty. I thought I had my goals nailed. "Stop and celebrate your success," a wiser colleague had suggested at the time. I didn't listen. I was intent on running up the corporate ladder as fast as I could–pushing myself as hard as I could. I wore my corporate suits like a shield, swinging my brief case as my sword, taking on each day ready for a fight. No matter how much I got pushed down, I rose up again swinging, trying to keep my emotion in autopilot. As a crisp career woman, I was experiencing professional success and my path for the future was clear. I thought I had it all figured out. I had all the answers.

A different story was unfolding at home where the real conflict was taking shape. My husband and I in a race to the top with two competing careers, who wanted to work late was often a source of tension. Cracks in our marital foundation took shape. We were financially strained with mortgage, car, and daycare payments. Our 2-year-old couldn't sleep through the night. Her insomnia became our shared exhaustion. Trying to keep up, I was walking the dog in the dark. He kept chewing my husband's favourite shoes. Looking back on that time, perhaps they were feeling the tension that blew through the house each night. Unable to express themselves in words, their actions yelled out for change. Life was a grind. The samurai warrior was feeling the strain. Some days we couldn't get to work fast enough.

But while things were a bit unsettled at home, professionally I thought it was blue skies and clear sailing ahead. Little did I know that there were clouds forming in the horizon and the perfect storm was on its way. Roaring into my life, it initially hit when I got fired. At the time, I had a high-profile job as public relations director for a well-known national retailer. The department I belonged to had undergone an organizational review. I was promised a position in the new organization, but on the day I learned my position was eliminated, I intuitively knew something was up. The meeting was scheduled weeks earlier, but the details surrounding its purpose were elusive. "I am going to get fired," I joked with a colleague as I left my office. "They wouldn't fire you," she reassured me. Entering my boss' office, he awkwardly greeted me with a human resources dude and a woman I didn't recognize sitting next to him. She was there to walk me out of the building. My time was up. Three against one–they represented a cast of thousands pushing me out the door. I drove home to share the news with my husband. He was shocked. My daughters, Kaileigh, then 3, and Sarah, 5, were thrilled.

When the full impact of losing my job unexpectedly fully engulfed me, it took my breath away. It would be a long time before I stood up again. "You can always go back in the future," my dad said when he eventually heard the news. "I will never go back," I declared.

Walking Sarah to school the next day, something I hadn't done since her first day of kindergarten, I got an unexpected lesson on perspective. "Hey everybody," Sarah exclaimed as we entered the playground. "This is my mom and she got fired! Yippee!" she yelled with glee, dancing around me in sheer delight. Nannies and stay-at-home moms stared. "Pavement swallow me up now!" I begged silently, just wanting to disappear in that moment. Looking around for moral support, I watched my samurai run in another direction.

My early definitions of "success" probably have a lot to do with my relationship with my dad. As my sister said at his funeral—"There is a little dad in all of us." My dad is why I am the corporate woman I am today. He was really a stranger to me as a child. I developed an appreciation for his professional and personal success as a young adult in business school. He was part of the Greatest Generation, having served as a Royal Canadian Air Force Spitfire pilot in World War II. On a mission, he was shot down over France and captured by Germans. He eventually escaped and made it to safety thanks to the French underground. "A great life adventure," he wrote in a telegram to his parents afterwards.

Thanks to his war experience, dad was able to pay for university, earning an Engineering degree from Queen's and later a Masters in Business Administration from Harvard. He went on to achieve a lifetime of success in business, government, and education. Dad had very high expectations of himself and those around him. A very competitive man, he loved a debate. You earned his respect by standing up to him. He spoke his mind and his words were powerful, sometimes painful. I respected him and loved him, while struggling to meet his expectations, perceived or real. I tried to mirror his experiences in my own life. I wanted to make him proud. "Don't embarrass me," he said, when I left the nest to pursue a career in corporate communications. His words ignited a fire within my gut. At that moment, I was determined to be a success. I would not disappoint him.

Losing my "forever" dream job triggered the beginning of a series of unfortunate events—many beyond my control—as the perfect storm played itself out. Both personally and professionally, I experienced unexpected loss and betrayal. Life around me was coming undone. I lost friendships I valued. My marriage was in crisis. We lost people we loved to unexpected illness. We were gradually losing my dad to Alzheimer's disease. He had become my coach and mentor. Using him as a sounding board, I sought his advice. The professional world was a shared interest we could talk about. All of the memories defining success for him would ultimately be eliminated by his illness. I was a helpless spectator, watching his life disappear like an image erased by time. There wasn't a thing I could do about it. Eventually, we lost him altogether when he passed over with no awareness of his achievements.

For me, getting back on the corporate ladder couldn't happen fast enough. Almost immediately after my initial job loss and without a lot of thought, I jumped on the first opportunity that came my way. It was a bad fit and I found myself falling back into unemployment. With two failed corporate positions following me around, it became almost impossible to keep my emotions reined in. "Mommy, why are you so sad?" my youngest asked. I started to unravel. I wanted to bolt. I kept pushing forward. Stuffing my grief and disappointment down, I desperately tried to master the art of disassociation, turning my back on my vulnerability. No matter how fast I moved and how much I did, eventually my emotions would catch up, tapping me on my shoulder when it was most inconvenient and unexpected. It could be a sunny day, but there was always a chance of tornado hitting unexpectedly, leaving a trail of debris. I found myself in the doctor's office complaining about the pain I felt everywhere—in my very core. After a series of tests he said: "I think you are depressed." "I am exhausted," I confessed, "I can't keep up. I am spinning out of control." Our girls were 4 and 6 at the time. He prescribed anti-depressants, but intuitively I knew that a bigger shift needed to occur for me to really feel well again.

During this period of unemployment, a friend invited me to accompany her to a Dude Ranch in Arizona. She would be participating in a conference and I could tag along for some personal leisure time. I could use this break to stop momentarily and take stock of my life. I hesitated to take it. Money was really tight by then. With my husband working overtime, I was leaving him alone at home to care for our two young girls knowing that our relationship was already tenuous and wrought with tension. He encouraged me to go. "I just want you to be happy," he said. Almost 20 years later, he still says that to me when I am down. Pretty low and feeling numb, I boarded the flight to Vegas.

Early in the trip I took an extended trail ride with a guide through the Sonoran Desert home to saguaro cactus. Having adapted to the harsh desert heat, surviving all that Mother Nature has thrown its way, this stately cactus is resilient and resourceful. It takes care of others, providing food and nesting sites for a variety of desert creatures. My inner samurai had found a kindred spirit in this magnificent symbol of the desert southwest.

Flowers of every colour and variety dotted the landscape, following a wet spring. Savouring the uniqueness of this spectacular experience, we rode by old saguaro cactus with big blue sky views of the horizon beyond. Fortunately, I was the only guest riding with the guide that day. For a while we rode in silence. On horseback together walking along through this beautiful desert, the silence moved in to an exchange of personal stories. Her life experiences gave me reason to pause. I opened my heart to her and allowed my vulnerability to pour out. She gave me some sage advice about family, relationships, and life in general. She married the cowboy. It didn't last. "Listen to your heart," she said. I did.

We ended our ride with a canter through a sandy washout. It was years since I had been on a horse at full throttle. I was nervous. "Are you ready for the ride of your life?" she said as she signalled her horse to move forward at a quicker pace. "Yes, let's do it," I said, letting go of my fear. I tossed my inhibition in the wind, hugged my knees to my horse, and followed her movement. Riding with abandon, we cheered out loud along the way. Exhilarated and breathless, I felt alive again.

I spent the following few days grazing over recent experiences. I realized that my marriage and children were more important to me than top spot on the corporate ladder. Work was important, but it didn't need to define me. Carving out a career that worked for me and making room for the needs of my family was my next step. I needed to take responsibility for my own career aspirations. Success no longer meant working for someone else to meet their expectations. That unexpected ride through the desert with horses and a wise woman, surrounded by the beauty and resilience of cacti where I released my fears to the universe, helped me make a decision to launch my own corporate communications and management consulting firm.

I called it The Cactus Group. The magnificent saguaro cactus became the symbol of my business, and ultimately it became the symbol of my professional success.

I was on the other side of this crisis and successfully self-employed a few years later when my husband and I purchased a century home in a small village 90 minutes away from the city. Six months after the purchase, we moved in full-time. This bold step wasn't really part of our "plan" at the time, but it felt right. My husband had landed a job in the area and I continued to work from home and commute to the city, juggling contracts between family commitments. It was an opportunity to exhale. It was the first step in a new direction for us.

On a visit from my parents, my dad and I shared a conversation that went like this: "You've made a mistake moving here. This is going to hurt your careers. There is no opportunity here. Your incomes will suffer. Your success will be limited," he said. "But we're happy," I said somewhat defensively, waking the samurai up, "I am happy. It's the right place for our family."

Like wet mud, his words stuck to me and I was never really able to brush them off. "You've made a mistake." In my heart, I knew that our decision to raise our family in the community we had chosen was the right one. We were defining success on our own terms. But I was still arguing with my samurai who believed that you could only achieve success in the city working downtown for someone else with a title that shouted professional achievement and awards that validated that achievement.

When I hit my forties, I was determined to try new experiences that took me out of my comfort zone and gave me reason to laugh. I wanted to put the loss I experienced earlier behind me, fully embracing life and those around me with an open heart. I knew that life was short. It was time to please myself as a woman rather than being someone who lived to meet the expectations of others.

I was inspired by a friend who had left her professional job to become an entrepreneur, establishing a women's wellness retreat. Listening to my creative soul, I signed up for a drum making workshop she offered. My crisp corporate self was learning to relax, come undone, and embrace a quirkier, creative me.

Horses found me again. My daughters and I took a year of horseback riding lessons together at a local stable. I loved this time with them. Then my youngest daughter Kaileigh and I travelled to Banff, Alberta to meet one of my sisters and her daughter for a four-day trip on horseback through the Canadian Rockies. The trip was a delayed celebration of milestone birthdays–my sister's 50th and my 40th.

I was thrilled to have this opportunity to share this real-life adventure with Kaileigh then 13-years-old before potentially losing her to adolescence. Travelling five-to-six hours per day up and down the crooks and crannies of Canada's backbone, we rode into the heart of the Rocky Mountains. We moved along in harmony with nature. The horses knew the trip and walked in single file accountable for their riders. Putting our trust in them, we fell into the rhythm of their step, moving forward for inclines and leaning back for declines. The footing was tricky in places as they led us safely through stunning scenery and difficult terrain. While the horses worked their magic, we caught up on life and enjoyed the camaraderie of the trail. Stunning scenery took our breath away. Memories of that special experience shared with people I love continue to give me reason to smile.

Life unfolded as it was meant to. My career carried on, my business continued to grow and with it my income. But I was still plagued by an undercurrent of doubt and insecurity. Was I the success I could be? Was dad right? His words still poked at my ego. Should I be doing more? Would I have had greater success living in the city?

Being just two years apart, our daughters both left the nest to attend university. Suddenly, the house was very quiet. After almost 20 years of focussing on others, I had found time that I didn't know what to do with. We could have downsized. Instead, my husband and I upsized and purchased a beautiful 80-acre farm. It was an "impulse" decision– not part of the "plan" but it felt right at the time. We called it Renegade Ridge Farm because as he noted: "We've taken a path less travelled." As a couple, it was a new start for us. We were on the cusp of hitting another new decade. Perhaps we were having a mid-life crisis. I believe we were having a mid-life awakening.

The property came with a barn, stalls, and pastures that seemed empty without animals. "I think I am going to buy a horse," I declared. Surprisingly my husband said he thought it was a good idea. While horses have carried me places throughout my life, I never expected to have one (or two) in my back yard. I knew very little if anything about them.

The ad read: "stunning palomino Tennessee Walker." Tennessee Walkers are a breed of gaited horses known for their quiet disposition, flashy movement, and unique four-beat "running walk." The picture of the horse featured in this online web site told another story. There he was covered in mud. He looked like a wild man, his mane and tail long, blonde and messy. He had a faraway, catch-me-if-you-can look. Sunny was his name and I wanted to meet him.

So on a cool, grey, rainy November day we took a drive to see Sunny. There he was in all his glory, surrounded by a few cows and a couple of horses in a pasture of mud and manure. He had not been ridden in a year. We walked him away from the herd closer to the barn for a trial ride.

That day, we threw a saddle on a horse that I knew very little about. I don't know what I was thinking or expecting from this experience, but I suppose that's how I'd always treated horses. It hadn't occurred to me that a much deeper partnership based on mutual respect could be achieved with these animals. Jumping on his back, we walked around the manure piles that dotted the field. He was pretty good for the first round and then the second. Then Sunny started to "dance" back towards the herd. I felt myself losing control. This was a new experience for me and I didn't know what to do. I am sure now Sunny sensed my uncertainty. "Take him around again," my husband said. I could feel the tension of Sunny's back between my legs. He was getting ready to run. "If you have any doubts, you should get down," his owner said. I got off and said I would take him. Sunny was my childhood Barbie horse in full flesh and blood. Little did I know then that this decision to buy a horse would turn out to be so life changing.

Jennifer on first ride with Sunny

My dad with his dog Blossom before heading overseas for WWII.

Jennifer and Kaileigh

*My sister Pat and my daughter Kaileigh (far left) riding through the
Canadian Rockies*

Sunny has a connection to my daughter Sarah

I had ridden a number of horses over the course of my life. Trail horses, lesson horses, and even a few owned by friends, they were all generally well-behaved and well-trained. They walked, trotted, and cantered on command. They didn't spook or bolt or at least not when I was on them. I thought I was a pretty decent rider, but there is a big difference between sitting on a well-trained horse and riding an inexperienced one. With Sunny's purchase, I would quickly learn how little I really knew about horses and how much they had to teach us. I was to be humbled in a really big way.

Since Sunny needed some "fine tuning" after living for a year without expectations, I sent him to a local trainer for a month. Thank goodness horses live in the moment as I had essentially sent him to boot camp after a year of living in leisure. "He's green," the trainer said, "He has a temper. He doesn't like new experiences. I don't think anyone has ever really worked with him." "He's probably in shock," I thought, hopeful he would have forgiven me by the time we met again.

On his "graduation day," Sunny and I took our first solo ride before going to a barn to board that winter. It was the first time I had ridden a horse without the company of others. I was nervous. I rode him around the track a few times, we walked back and forth across a bridge, and we went for our first trail ride together. Sunny had learned the route and knew what to do. We arrived back to the barn safe and sound. A walk through a stream completed our adventure. We stopped in the water and in that moment, captured on camera by my husband, I felt honoured to be in the presence of this wonderful being. It was magical. Having Sunny was an unexpected dream come true for me. He was still a mystery to me, but our initial journey together was a successful one. I felt empowered. When we left the farm, I was on a personal high.

A large indoor riding arena was waiting for us at the boarding facility. Full of anticipation and expectation the next day, I went back to the barn to take Sunny out for our first ride. My husband came along for moral support.

As we walked into the arena, Sunny seemed nervous and jumpy. It hadn't occurred to me that perhaps he had never been in an arena before and this was a new experience for him. There were other riders and horses already there. I took Sunny over to the mounting block so I could get on. He danced around and wouldn't stand still. So my husband held him while I mounted up. Amidst the other riders, I was feeling self-conscious and nervous. I wanted to make a good first impression. Stepping away from the mounting block, Sunny and I were almost immediately assaulted by the sound of snow sliding off the arena roof. This highly amplified sound of fingernails scratching down a giant chalkboard made me jump. It made Sunny jump even higher.

Sunny jerked sideways and almost fell to the ground in fear. I held on for life desperate to stay on while trying to keep my composure in an arena that had now fallen silent as everyone watched. Frozen in fear, Sunny refused to move forward, his lower lip quivering. I jumped off. Never had I experienced a horse spooking before and little did I know then that this would be one of many spooks I'd experience while riding him. His well-developed instinct for flight would ultimately earn him the title: Sunny with a Chance of Tornado.

"Get back on him," my husband, who had not been up on a horse for many years, said. My samurai raised her sword in his direction and screamed in my head: "You get on him!" as I tried to remain calm while the other riders looked on sympathetically. One woman in particular, who would later become a valued friend and coach, came to my aid. "If you have any doubts, stay on the ground and try again tomorrow," she said. I took her advice. We led Sunny back to the cross-ties, unsaddled him, put him in his stall and went home. Then I cried. Feeling humiliated and defeated, my samurai started to rock in the fetal position. What was I thinking?! It was in this moment that I realized the leap of faith I had taken with my investment in this horse. How little I knew about horses in general and Sunny in particular. Successfully setting us both up for failure, we experienced it together.

Returning to the barn for my second ride, I was determined to take a different approach the next day. The arena was empty; weather calm. Sunny had settled a bit in his new environment. I spent some time grooming him and getting acquainted. Walking him around the arena a few times, I introduced him to his surroundings before getting on him. We had a quiet ride. He didn't spook. I didn't fall off. There was hope for us. Then I made a commitment to learn as much about horses as I could and to get to know Sunny better before expecting so much from him.

I discovered a group of like-minded women who rode in the evenings, timing my ride to coincide with theirs. Sunny and I became part of the circle, concluding each ride in the middle of the area for story telling. We took lessons together.

Saying goodbye to Sunny each night, I left more relaxed then when I arrived. I had to be fully present and mindful when working with him, anticipating his moves, and providing leadership along the way. This connection meant that I had to let go of the mind-full of "stuff" I had collected each day—expectations, worries, and to-do lists. My time with him became unexpected therapy and stress management. Both mentally and physically, I became a healthier person. I looked forward to my arrival at the barn and each moment I spent with my horse. I had found an outlet that appealed to and engaged all dimensions of my being—intellectually, emotionally, intuitively, and spiritually. I had found my passion.

I voraciously read as many books about horses as I could. Leadership, self-awareness, and mindfulness were common themes. As I had ample leadership development opportunities in my professional life working with others, these concepts were not new to me. They did, however, take on a higher level of meaning as I was working with a 1,200 pound horse that had a well-developed need to flee with me on his back.

The magic of working with these sentient beings began to emerge. I knew that if I was going to calm Sunny's fears then I needed to take control of my own fears and embrace the shadows that followed me into the arena every night. I needed to be mindful of what was happening with my own emotions. I had to regulate the ebb and flow of my own Chi or life force. My samurai was learning to swim and splash in the emotional river that flowed just below the surface of my competent, strong professional self.

Perhaps it was time to make peace with my emotions, embrace them, and learn from them. Author Linda Kohanov's advice was to "let an experience move you to the core rather than disassociate from it, perhaps leaving you raw and vulnerable for a time, yet ultimately strengthen your ability to embrace life fully and consciously, inspiring others in the process."[1] It was advice I needed to hear.

Perhaps it was fate that I first learned about the FEEL (Facilitated Equine Experiential Learning) Certification program offered by Horse Spirit Connections at a drumming circle. When the talking stick was passed to me, I found myself babbling like a wild woman, openly sharing the unexpected experiences and personal awakening that was unfolding with my growing herd of horses. Another participant shared her experience with the FEEL program offered by Horse Spirit Connections.

Intrigued, I checked out their web site. I called Horse Spirit Connections Founder Wendy Golding, arranging to meet with her. She said the horses were calling me. I wasn't convinced that was true but I was reassured by her corporate experience and success that preceded her decision to work with horses as teachers full-time. Perhaps this wasn't some crazy midlife crisis after all. I could see the value of working with horses to gain self-knowledge and acquire skills that lead to greater self-awareness and positive life changes. I could see how much my relationship with Sunny (and seven other horses filling our stalls) had caused me to pause and reflect upon the way I lived, responding with sharper awareness to the world around me. I could see the benefits of using horses for team building and leadership development in the corporate world and the medical community where my consulting work took me. It all felt right to me. My heart wanted to jump in with both feet; my head suggested I walk before I run.

After participating in a FEEL workshop with my husband, I enrolled in the FEEL certification program. As a successful communications and management consultant, I could see the possibility of complementing my existing work with a horse-focused initiative that created opportunity for personal and professional development. I put my focus on getting the certificate with this intent. Working with the program's horses as my own personal teachers was an unexpected and underestimated benefit. Even with the personal insights I had gathered from Sunny, I must admit that I entered that first week of the program with some degree of doubt and skepticism. My red flags went up when Wendy started to talk about horse ancestors and how the horses communicated with one another. Some of the concepts introduced were a bit out there for my comfort zone. In fact, some of them freaked me out. Were horses really that perceptive? Could they be facilitators of change? A practical person, I had, however, paid the price of admission so I was committed to completing the program. I was soon to get a big spoonful of the unexpected medicine a jet black horse named Paris had in store for me.

Concurrently that summer, I was mindful of all the feathers I started to notice on our property. I became aware of them leading the horses from one spot to another—in the paddock, near the barn, on the road—they seemed to be everywhere. Feathers are a gift from the spirit world, a friend shared. Feathers reflect the fact that no matter what physical obstacles are put in our way during our life's journey, we all have the ability to rise above our fears and limitations, and, in doing so, we will be able to rise to new levels of understanding. I took note of this message and I began to incorporate my found feathers into my artwork.

As part of the FEEL training, a number of exercises would follow that gave me reason to believe in the power of possibility. The horses had some surprises in store for me. One of the activities that shook my reality was a Spiritual Journey Ride on horseback. The intent of this Shamanic technique is to reveal, release, and transform the patterns and barriers that inhibit and stifle a person's growth and create an opening for their creative energies.

My intent going into this unique "ride" was to let go of expectations. I was still being haunted by a few ghosts from my past. I intuitively knew that until I released myself from a definition of success and the expectations of others that no longer fit the person whom I'd become–I would not be able to move forward with purpose into the next phase of my life.

Paris was my partner on this trip. I was drawn to Paris when we first met the herd. I had then experienced her "magic" on a number of occasions, learning to trust in the wisdom she offered along the way. I can only describe my Spiritual Journey Walk with Paris as a very personal one that can't be limited by words on a page. When it was complete, I asked the facilitator if I could give Paris a hug before leaving her back. I wanted to thank her for sharing this experience with me. As I put my head down on her neck and took in a breath of her musky coat, I found myself sobbing into her warm flesh. I came undone. Like vomit, repressed grief, disappointment, and profound sadness came spewing out of my mouth. I would later call this "my Green Mile" moment. Paris remained still and accepted what I had to share. I had embraced my shadow self. The intensity of the moment was unexpected. I was shocked by it. My vulnerability was on full display. I would need time to process this overwhelming surprise. But I knew I felt lighter. I felt light as a feather.

Sometimes success is an unexpected gift or surprise. A few weeks later, I was describing my experience with Paris to a friend and business colleague. She and I had previously discussed the impact our dads had on our professional life, and we had a shared appreciation for their influence. "What was your father's relationship with Paris?" she asked unexpectedly. "I don't know," I said, pausing for the first time to reflect on a potential connection. "The only thing I can think of is his experience in World War II. He could have lost his life in France as a prisoner of war. When I was going through his belongings, I found a picture of him in the *Globe and Mail* from 1944. The caption read: 'French women of Caen fill the glasses of Canadian airman with brandy following their arrival in the newly liberated Normandy city, former Nazi stronghold.' They were celebrating the war's end."

"Think about the words that you are sharing in this moment. Your dad is sending you a message. The war is over. It's time to celebrate." She was right. It was insight I hadn't even considered until that moment. It was time to let go of some of my own dated definitions of success and the need to meet the expectations of others including my dad, real or perceived I had attached to it. It was time to celebrate my own personal and professional success. My experience with Sunny and the other horses that have crossed my path have taught me that success is not about the goal or the outcome. Success is about the wisdom collected on the way along the trail to your destination. Success is about savouring each moment every step of the way. It was time to put my sword down and to hug my samurai. It was time to make peace with myself and the demons that followed me.

When you work with horses over a period of time, it becomes clear that each horse and each person experiences the other uniquely on their own terms. Working with horses as teachers, each activity has a clear goal, but no two experiences are the same. The journey and the insight gained along the way is the reward and that reward carries a different message and meaning to each individual.

Similarly, success means different things to different people. Horses connect people to possibility. When I look back at my dad's life and all that he accomplished, I realize that he was a person who lived life fully with intent. He wanted only what was best for himself and his family. His perceptions, actions, and words were shaped by his own experiences. But you can't live someone else's life for them. Nor should you allow the expectations of others to limit what's possible. Horses are teaching me to define and create success on my own terms by taking the lead and believing in what's possible. Thanks to my dad and the Greatest Generation he was part of, we each have the freedom to use the power of our mind to choose our own thoughts, feelings, and growth directions; to go with our gut; and follow our heart's desire.

When my professional life began, I envisioned a life living in the city working for someone else. I never envisioned a life living on a farm with horses. Nor did I envision having my own business. Neither reality is a bad thing. It's just not what I expected. It is clearly where I am meant to be, and it is a life far richer than anything I could have pictured for myself so many years ago.

I also never thought that I would be launching a new venture–The Mane Intent, my own FEEL program, offered up to connect people to possibility through horse power. It's a venture that represents a culmination of many life experiences–personal and professional. It's the next step in my walk with horses. Our intent is to help others discover ways to nurture and strengthen interpersonal connections, find connection, and meaning in a busy life, unearth personal talents, gifts, and creativity, and live life fully with an open heart. It's the kind of work I am putting my own heart into.

Today, I am living my own life fully with intent. Horses are a big part of that. Author Caroline Myss has written: "Just let go. Let go of how you thought your life should be, and embrace the life that is trying to work its way into your consciousness."[2] For me, that means the forecast is sunny with a chance of tornado. For that I am grateful. Bring it on.

Jennifer Garland

Jennifer Garland is a certified FEEL Practitioner and Founder/Lead Facilitator of The Mane Intent Inc. (www.themaneintent.ca), connecting people to possibility through horse power using facilitated equine experiential learning. Jennifer brings to this unique work over 25 years of leadership experience in communications, marketing, and change management for a variety of sectors including healthcare. The focus of her professional life as Founder/President of The Cactus Group is developing strategic relationship building approaches for individuals, executive teams, and the organizations they lead by drawing upon her unique combination of facilitation, organizational change, and marketing communications and community investment experience. Her consulting work includes providing counsel and support to senior leaders to create opportunities to build productive relationships, facilitate learning, and to embrace change. Complementing a diploma in public relations and a degree in Business Admin/Political Science, Jennifer has a Certificate in Managing Strategic Change and a Certificate in Conflict Resolution and Mediation.

Away from the office and out of the barn, Jennifer is an avid gardener, nature lover, and mixed media artist believing in the reincarnation of found objects and images. In 2001, she and her family said goodbye to city living and embraced country life. Shortly after their purchase of Renegade Ridge Farm in 2011, Jennifer purchased her first horse, Sunny (with a Chance of Tornado). Today the farm boasts a growing herd of wonderful horses, a few goats, dogs, and other creatures. With its large perennial gardens and history, the farm offers the perfect setting for individuals, teams and small groups to explore what's possible, while connecting with horses and nature.

CHAPTER 10

How Much We Can Love

By Kera Willis

I bought my first horse when I was 17. A serious, warrior mare who came to me with the name Bush Pig, given for her love of jumping fences. I renamed her Mree, after a gelding in *The Horse and His Boy*[1]. She carried me through three years of apprenticeship in eventing and dressage, and never surrendered her love of freedom. At a German dressage barn she taught herself to *Capriole*, leaping 4 feet in the air with all of her legs tucked up under her belly like a silver grey torpedo, aimed directly at my coach. She snuck through lines of electric fence by wedging her thick mane under the top wire, lifting it up, and carefully stepping her legs over the bottom wires. She jumped out of box stalls, cleared 5 foot rail fences while her pasture mates grazed nonchalantly, and once let a friend's herd out for a walkabout by bending a series of T-posts sideways with the belly straps of her turnout rug. She carried me across moonlit fields with no tack on her; just a young woman lying with her arms spread, opening her heart to the sky. She carried me into rivers and swam, emerged with her coat darkened to steel grey, my boots soaked, and dripping with river weed.

It's funny that out of all of the horses who have rafted alongside my life, it is she who returns to carry me now. She comes to me in the way that dreams come, feathering against the threshold of awareness. If she is still alive, it is somewhere far from my physical life.

But sometimes she calls to me with the mysterious gravity of a dream, tugging my attention across the borders that lie between worlds. The language she speaks is soul language, older than the mountains that stand guard over my life.

I gift her crow feathers. She is pleased that I can recognize her for exactly what she is: a granite-warrior mare gone white with age; who has softened into gentleness without giving away any of her strength. Together we stand at the edge of the ocean, snort the salt air into our lungs, and lower our muzzles as we step into the waters of this story.

The world is old and will be older still when we are finished. Before there are still birds in the sky. Before the karma of the story passes us through the eye of the needle and unravels us.

It was his horse that I passed on the road. Levade. Pesade. Ballotade. Every movement he taught me how to train was once for war.

Mezair. Croupade. Terre-a-Terre. These words are spells, the lost names for ancient equine battle maneuvers called airs above the ground that gave aristocrats the ability to train wings into their horses. Wings that would enable them to soar through the fields of battle and escape the enemy swords.

Falling asleep these past few nights I've felt the edges of our long ago lives pressing against my consciousness; a sliver in the foot that with every step, makes itself known.

This is the first life in which I choose not to fight him. Before this, our histories were all stories of clashes, battle songs sung round the fires late at night. In some lives we were lovers. In others I stood

on top of hills and watched his army turn against mine. His people slaughtered my people. My people slaughtered his people. Mist rose from the hillsides, smoke from the fires that cleared the fields after battle. Even in this life when I touched his hands they were curled, as if they still held weapons. The answer to any conflict was still war.

And I loved him, yes: The way a dog still takes food from a bowl held by a hand that may, at any moment, hit him.

How war paces the boundaries of love.

I came here to marry worlds. I began my life with horses as a rider, and when I left the sport world—in the years I spent exploring Equine Guided Learning and other ways of being with horses—I felt like I had lost a portion of my power. While I believed that the healing I witnessed and experienced was real, I did not know how to share it from the ground. Everything I knew that could gift wings was something I could only fathom teaching from the back of a horse. In the summer of 2013 I left for Texas to do an apprenticeship in Horse Boy Method[2]: a genius fusion of classical dressage, therapeutic riding, kinetic learning, and an immersion in the natural world designed specifically for work with autism and other neurological disorders. In some readings of the bones, I would have stayed down there forever. But one bone, the trickster bone, the one that is coyote, sent me back to howl on the flat rock of the Canadian Shield, to ride between the edges of the unknown and the known.

"Autism is deep love... Autism is being able to be consumed by love...it is giving 100% because it is an insult to the thing to give it any less."

-Neurodivergent K[3]

Their hearts as large as horses.

"Kerance!

"Kerance!"

Alex talks with a full glee grin, his intakes of breath straight inhalations of joy, as if joy existed outside of his body and had to be swallowed whole in order to be experienced. It is an intensity that makes my heart leap to be in its presence; that reminds me, in an instant, who and where I am. This.

He is running. Calling out his particular name for me: a mongrel of my own and another young woman's; a thin Parisian named Marie-Laurence.

Marie-Laurence boosts him up into the saddle in front of me. We're riding a horse named Marvel, a big-going gelding who can canter on the spot in a long-forgotten movement called *Terre-a- Terre;* intended to ready the horse for an attack in hand-to-hand combat. We use it with autistic kids because it releases euphoric feelings in the body, a particular kind of Oxytocin-fuelled bliss that drops stress instantly, and heals the brain. I could give you the science of it. I could rap to you about hormones, reducing inherently high cortisol levels, creating resonance ,and heart-brain coherence, and the healing effects of movement. But simply, this is the one day a week when Alex has wings.

"Marvel have boogers?" Alex wants to know. Marie-Laurence checks. "No, not today."

"Kerance has BLUE eyes." Alex turns around in the saddle to check. Looks into my eyes with an intensity that is almost too much to bear, and then throws his arms around my neck. A stranglehold. For a moment the world disappears. I am being held by an ocean, the roots of an ancient tree run long underground. Then he lets me go.

"Marvel, CANTER!" A request. I tip my weight onto my right seat bone, move my left heel back, declare "canter!" and the gelding does; through the woods along a trail that when it rains becomes a river alive with floodwater, depositing fish into the branches of the trees. I hold the gait's collection between my shoulder blades, make the steps shorter/

shorter/ shorter yet the power more; all of this in an instant before we clatter against the base of the hill and turn left along another creek bed, looking for where Marie-Laurence has hidden a plastic hippopotamus. Alex has gone quiet in the saddle in front of me, soaking it all in. But his face is alive, awake, aware. Flying.

If I listen very carefully I can pick up the track of his life, moving on the other side of the world: can hear the quick steps of the stallion he is riding fresh out of the gate, its steel grey coat already gone wet with sweat.

I hold open the gates that let them out into the world because I want to and not because I am needed. Beyond the gates of the stallion pens, I watch them Piaffe under the limbs of the oak trees, the stallion trots almost completely on the spot, his rider perfectly still like some ancient depiction of a king or a god. He turns to me and says: "The only way any of us are here is because of love."

Love for lifetimes or for an instant; the long draw reins of devotion or the pure brilliant flash. There was sheet lightning in the sky at midnight the first night I came here. Rain on the wind minutes later. The smell of the wet ground was somehow familiar, and I stood out in the night for a long time trying to place it. Trying to find the thread of some long-ago story that would tell me I had been here before. I recognized him in an instant, though I did not know then how far back the lineages went. That I had kissed him between the walls of canvas tents on battlefields gone wet with moonlight while our opposing armies slept, the dogs even too exhausted to give cry. That in this life we would turn against each other too, with a particular kind of cruelty.

And yet, and yet.

The horses that carry us are still doing the same work in the world.

We are only ever here because of love.

When I first encountered autism, it was in Linda Kohanov's book *The Tao of Equus*[4]. The book found me exactly when I was ready for it. In a few brief pages, she describes an encounter with Charles, an older man she worked with in a group home, who was deaf with autistic tenancies. This is when Linda was just beginning to flesh out the concepts of authenticity, congruence, and resonance that would go on to form the bedrock of her teachings. She wrote:

> *I decided to try a little wu wei* [a Japanese concept that translates as literally "not doing"] *with my quiet friend... I turned the TV off, sat across from Charles, and stared into space. As my breathing slowed, the rising and falling of Charles' chest became deeper and more relaxed in response. A few minutes later I began to notice tiny, multifaceted lights dancing through the room, as if I was seeing the air. I smiled at Charles, delighted. He smiled back. An incredible wave of ecstasy filled my body. Was I resonating with Charles on a similar frequency?...I looked at Charles. Tears were streaming down the cheeks of his numinous face. My eyes too began to sting... We hugged briefly in the centre of the room.*

> *"Thank you for showing me your secret world." I signed. "Secret world." He echoed back with the subtlest of movements.*

> *- Linda Kohanov*[4]

Kohanov's encounter became a gestalt: a perspective of openness and possibility I carried with me that deeply influenced the way I approach persons with special needs. The FEEL work informed my life in much the same way, becoming the bedrock of the way I go about being with horses, the way I bring humans and horses together, the way I choose to be human. When I completed my certification in 2010, Wendy Golding asked me: "What are you going to do now?"

"Teach people how to be autistic." I said, without thinking. But it was true: I wanted to teach people how to be authentic, congruent, intuitive, and heart-centric; to reconnect them to the wild heart of the natural world, and to enable them to feel, really feel, what the depths of what their lives are offering in every present moment. But I meant it literally too: I wanted to teach parents and allies of autistic people how to slip into an autist's world, how to open to a different way of being that is as foreign to us as a horse's. Because autism is not about savants or spectrums, ABA or cures; it's not about memorizing particular train schedules or pages of the stock exchange or redesigning slaughterhouses or being more comfortable in the company of animals, it's about making an offering. It's about cultivating openness ripe as a temple from which you can turn to another human and meet them in their moment entirely. It's about the fierce desire that together you can burn a doorway into the rock that has grown between you and the world. It's about opening our hearts and minds to other ways of being; other, wilder ways of sensing and interpreting life as it moves through us. It's about recognizing the interconnectedness and advocacy of every single living thing, because it is only within these relationships that we become whole.

Working with autism is about finding a doorway and asking, humbly, to be let in. It's about realizing the person in the saddle in front of you has just given themselves to you entirely and in fact always has; they have entered into your life as far as they have been able. Now it is your turn to trade that gift and meet them at least halfway. To leave the barriers of what you know behind and accept purely what is. It is as if this acceptance is a lens that tunes your heart and mind and only now do you see rightly, with anything akin to truth. And more than seeing, you begin to feel the world. Sometimes with an acuity that is almost unbearable, and sometimes with a sensation of softness, as if you are being held, by some great benevolence beyond your fathoming.

It is the horses, also, that gift us this shared perspective. A clairsentience that, like an empathogen, allows us to see the connectedness of all things. And in saying "connectedness" I really mean love; I really mean the scarred wooden door that guards your own heart falling away, leaving you permeable, multifaceted, existing in reciprocal relationship with everything you touch. This is what autism teaches us. What being with horses teaches us. This is the territory we carried us to.

The horses come to me clinking their bits between their teeth. Their eyes are the colour of green glass, the skin that covers their muzzles so thin it must be permeable. Their eyes flash like screens playing something I need to see: the moment I stood in the kitchen and lied to him with what I hoped was confidence, my eyes finding his like arrows, black stones knowing their way home. I don't know whether he chose to believe me, or whether he tucked this moment into his back pocket to use against me later, the way he would watch a horse rear in defiance or pain and smile, knowing that a year from now he would be able to channel this expression into a Levade and knock his opponent down, pin his soul against the sky. I held his gaze as he walked out of the kitchen. By the time his arm brushed mine I was unflinching. Committed.

This moment that passed between us was more ancient then today's story. It has happened again and again in other lives, messengers carrying torches up to the commanders at the front lines, shouting into slaughter-drunk ears that the moment is ripe to turn the lines of battle. It opened up a new front through the middle of our allied fighting. I watched it spread like a tear in the fabric that rippled up against the bottom of the hill where I stood. I could

see him on the other side of the valley, mounted on a grey stallion standing perfectly motionless. Across the distance our eyes locked. Turning our armies against each other.

"I think that people with autism are born outside of the regime of civilization... We are more like travellers from the distant, distant past. And if, by our being here, we could help the people of the world remember what truly matters for the earth, that would give us a quiet pleasure."

– Naoki Higashida[5]

It is cold in Texas. Marie-Laurence, Liz, Amber, and I spend the week burning brush in the woods. A family comes in from the UK and someone they meet at a gas station gives them all winter coats.

"I guess it really is true" the woman says. "What they say about Southern hospitality." She is tall, with long black hair. Her husband's face I do not remember.

Their 6-year-old son is in the saddle in front of me. We are riding Betsy under the tin roof of the covered arena, but the wind that blows in from the northeast is still freezing. The boy refuses to wear the jacket that was given to him, and his hands have gone red with cold. I send Tom up to the house for a soft blanket and a tiny hot water bottle we were given to keep a sick rabbit warm. By now the war is in full swing and I am not allowed to give orders but the boy is cold, and so I do it anyways. When Tom returns I wrap the blanket over the boy's shoulders and put the warmth of the hot water bottle into his hands. He holds onto it gently keeping it perfectly upright, as if it were a bird.

Under us Betsy's heart beats a much slower rhythm, as if it belonged to the earth itself. The boy is in the saddle in front of me, wrapped in a blanket. I canter with one arm around his shoulders to steady him; halt, turn, canter again. I am searching through movement for a key; a way to open the door that exists between us. Around the edges of the ring the girls have lit fires and huddle beside them to keep warm. I am reminded of walking in the desert late at night, through darkness absolute and cold as deep lake water, and coming to a fire ringed with warmth and human faces. Hello. I am of you. I am not of you. Ricocheting between the polarities.

I halt Betsy in the centre of the ring and stand waiting, waiting for something to tell me what to do. By now I know that this will be my last day here. The fires lit around the edges of the arena are burning the last of my dead. We have created this ritual for this boy, but it is also for me too. The lines the chain harrow has left in the sand under us are the marks of the battlefield being raked clean.

The wind gusts in from the North and parts around us as if we were a boulder in the middle of a mountain stream. Betsy stands with her ears at half mast, every string in her tuned towards us. We wait.

"He's watching the wind move up in the trees," the boy's mother says. I follow the tilt of his head that tells me that his gaze has sailed up into the tops of the oak trees. I can feel the solid whoosh of the wind, feel it blowing the bones of the oak's bare branches. The utter emptiness between every living thing. And yet, at the same time, proximity. I watch the green leaved branches toss in gusts that we do not feel on the ground yet are happening all around us. And there, in that moment, is the doorway: the gift that lets us shape shift into each other's worlds. The horse and the tree and the boy who is the wind, a woman on an ancient horse becoming still in the eye of the storm. Somehow the boy takes me up there with him. Up into the wild gusts, where everything is free and clean and fresh with velocity, up into the pure potentiality of air.

Just as suddenly as the shift happened, the wind dies. I come back into a body that is holding reins that connect me to the mind of a horse, and the blanket-wrapped shoulders of a very cold 6-year-old boy.

"Let's go to the house and get warmed up," I say to his mom. Just once, the boy turns in the saddle and looks at me. He does not smile. His face is expressionless. But his eye goes on and on, is bottomless. Seeing me.

Birds fly in from the East, thousands of them? "Here, here, here" their voices call to their mates. "Where are you?" "Here."

And seconds later. "Where are you?"

"Still here."

Kera and kids

Mirror

Confluence

Kera at the chief estuary

The birds pour like liquid flying a highway in the air, a like mountain stream ripe with running Chinook salmon flung into the sky above my head. I walk towards their path of flight and the line in the sky bends away from me like a guitar string forcing a note up a semitone. I backtrack my steps and the line straightens out; moves back to its original place. What is it that tells them that I am here; what resonance is it that announces my movement through all these legions of wild air? To these birds the air is alive, potent as a headline.

I dance with them like this. Moving back and forth across the lawn at 6:30 a.m., bending curves into a line of birds flying with such perfect velocity that as soon as one has passed over my head it is replaced by another, and another, and another, each bird potent with its own cry, shouting "here, here, here," flying on and on to who knows where, out beyond the thousand things we cannot see.

So our many lives move with us.

When I leave Texas, it takes me four days of hard driving to get back up to Canada. I choose Ontario as a landing place because of a dream; a dream and a stone. So thin is my hold on the world. The stone is a Moqui Marble, a round composite of iron and sandstone also called a Shaman's Stone, because they were often carried in medicine bundles by people who garnered their magic from the arid plains of the American Southwest. A man named Ron Kulker gave me one that Texas summer, and when I decide that I am going to walk away from the battle, the rain brings more up out of the ground.

Every time I look down I find another marble. They are shaped like bullets, dense. As more and more fall into my heart, I let them tell me where to go. The dream is more complex. In it, I am lying on the back of a great horse, a mare so large her body becomes the earth. Ron is holding her lead rope as I lie back on her rump and spread my arms to the sky. Hummingbirds swoop in above me, so many that the whirring of their wings becomes a cloud. One hovers just above my face and drips nectar into my eyes that fall down my cheeks as tears. Another pierces the skin of my finger and drinks. The bird at my finger is such a sharp agony, and the one at my eyes causes such a soft wave of release that the contrast is too much, and I slide off the mare, helped by hands onto the ground where I rest, still guarded, still protected, still perfectly held.

Halfway through my time in Ontario I am sitting bareback on the Dass Mare. She is 17.2 hands high; huger than huge, with a spooky eye and a wise heart. I lie on her rump with my arms spread out towards the sky, flying my heart back into the world. A sweetness rises up from the mare and holds me within it, bursts in my heart with such softness I think I will cry. And this flighty, spooky mare holds me perfectly, collapsed in a sweetness I barely understand; cherry blossoms on an East Vancouver street, the feeling in the air just after someone has died. It was the feeling from my dream. Somehow, I had chosen rightly.

I spend 6 months with Ron and his wife Suzie, helping to create the *Heal With Horses Therapeutic Centre*[6], offering FEEL work and Horse Boy Method sessions in Prince Edward County, Ontario. When I arrived, Suz was just beginning to transition her herd of FEEL horses into doing more riding-based autism work, and my job was to see who—out of 11 richly storied characters—wanted to emerge as safe riding horses. But we needed more than safe riding horses: we needed horses who would willingly join us on adventures, who could take the physical work of carrying two riders, and who would say yes to anything while still keeping their soul intact. That time has its share of holy moments too: birds flying overhead. Gifts of wings.

Come, come. I will take you up to the shattered rim of the world, and I will bring you back.

Whole.

"We need another wiser and perhaps more mystical concept of animals... In a world older and more complete than ours, they move finished and complete, gifted with the extension of the senses we have lost or never attained, living by voices we shall never hear. They are not brethren, they are not underlings: they are other nations, caught with ourselves in the net of life and time, fellow prisoners of the splendour and travail of the earth."

- Henry Beston[7]

There is another boy. Braydon. Like a huge and ancient horse, everything about him is absolute. You could be walking and talking, not paying any attention and then when you come up close to him you are forced to stop. Your mind bounces off him. Like a mountain, you need to let his silence take you in.

He taught me how much I was still not listening. How if we come at this work with even a hint of an agenda, we are not listening. Even if we dress our agenda up to look like an adventure, or a game of tag, or a scavenger hunt, it is still an agenda. It is still imposing our version of the world on another with very little concern for what we might be missing. Braydon taught me all of this without saying a word. He quietly sat down and put his hand into the water of the creek. We were catching tadpoles, and Amy and I were whisking about with pails and nets, talking about frogs' life cycles, finding tadpoles with various stages of legs and showing them to Braydon. He said nothing. He was tolerating us. Amusing us. And then he sat down in the mud and put his hand into the water of the creek. And waited.

I put my hand into the creek and waited too. I wanted to see what would happen. And we waited. And waited. I watched the squiggling black forms moving in the water, and saw them. Really saw them. Not as a progression in some science textbook, not as a named, categorizable and therefore dismissible thing, but simply for what they were: black dots with tails, animate and alive in ways that seemed impossible, worthy exactly as they were and not for something they would become. They had mouths and two golden eyes on top of their heads and they would swim close to the edges of our hands and then loose their nerve and swim away. Braydon waited. I waited. And then they started swimming into the palms of our hands. If you lifted your hand in a certain way with your fingers spaced a certain distance apart, you could lift the tadpole out of the water and have a look at it in that strange way humans do by holding things close to our faces. Braydon was lifting each one and looking at it with great care, and then—in precisely the right amount of time, before the tadpole drowned in air—he returned it to the water, and then left his hand there and waited for another tadpole. And when he was done he simply got up and walked away.

There is something in quantum physics that says that whenever a person has touched us part of their DNA stays on our bodies where the skin has made contact; that it takes seven years for the tracer lights of that connection to die. And so we are always leaving ourselves on others; even if it is just the wind; blowing us away to somewhere else entirely.

"Lay the weapon down" the white mare says to me, over and over, as if it were an incantation.

"Lay the weapon down."

There are no other clues.

I have a dream in which he comes into the shed that was my home those slender months, climbs up the ladder in the dark and lies down in bed beside me. Puts his left arm across my shoulders and kisses me on the cheek.

He says nothing and I cannot see him in the darkness. But the feeling of the kiss stays with me even as I wake: permanent, as if it were a word.

By the time you are reading this I will have taken up the reins again and galloped home: driven 4,885 kilometres around the northern shore of Lake Superior, through Calgary's towers of newly monied steel and glass, through a slip spot in the spine of the Rockies called Kicking Horse Pass, and then flown through the sage and sun of the interior of BC. I will have passed through Vancouver, traveled over the Lions Gate Bridge, and up along the shining corridor of Howe Sound. I will have clocked my last kilometres on the fresh drawn line of the Sea to Sky Highway, pulled like a thread between the edge of the mountains and the edge of the sea as it moves inland, potent with dolphins and killer whale.

And finally, at the confluence—where the shining silver corridor of the Squamish River meets the salt of Howe Sound—I will have stood, and taken a breath; and watched the entirety of my life roll in to meet me. Churches and medicine wheels and mosques and temples, bonfires and hailstorms and river stones and wind. Those that I have wounded and those that I have healed: those who have wounded me once and then again when I came back for more. Those I have lifted up and those I've let pass through me like wind, like water, to unravel their fates on someone else. And always, always, the horses: Horses that have pulled ploughs, wagons, stagecoaches; horses that have jumped high and run fast, carried letters, outlaws, lovers. Horses that have come to me with gifts, their dark eyes saying "listen."

Listen. I can show you the way forward and the way back. I hold a mirror for you in this moment.

What do you to see?

At my feet and above my head walk, run, fly the animals who have made themselves present in all my dreams of human lives: buffalo, owl, raven,

crow, leopard, and a whole string of unmounted horses that choose me as their rider. When I am still I can hear the sound of their hooves, tracking up to mine. Waiting to become still.

Some of the horses have other riders, members of an ancient army. Some of the members of the armies who rode with me on ancient battlefields are still with me now; a line of coloured stragglers sewn into my life so strongly that the thread has become invisible. The stitching on their battle clothes has loosened, and birds use the threads they find on the wind to make their nests. In the realms where they move, there is never not a horse under me. Beside the soles of our bare feet, there will never not be a horse print. Whenever we move there will always be the sound of hooves.

They, too, have decided to walk away from the fight. To put their energy instead into creating what is possible. The armour they used to wear has long fallen off their bodies and rusted back into the land from which it came; becoming mineral, earth, stone. I cannot see them in their entirety. Sometimes I catch a glimpse of a forearm or wrist, a braid flying over a shoulder, the billowing once-ornate fabric that makes up their clothes, a horse's moving ear. A hoof the colour of river stone.

When I am still I can hear the sound of their hooves, tracking up to mine. Wolves howling from the fringes of the trees. And they press up against my back, drive me out and out and out into the mossy cathedrals of old growth cedars, into the fields that have gone wild without us, out into a celebration of birdsong, a scatter of small tracks and dark eyes.

I am not sure where the road leads from here.

The line of the highway falls off the edge of the map; has been dissolved by a river. What I know: that a friend has bought land, deep in the heart of the Upper Squamish Valley in BC, and that from there, I will grow roots.

In the spring of 2015 I will begin to offer sessions under the name Mountain Horse School. Sessions for autistic kids, and also what I have begun calling "encounters"; experiences that are a fusion of ridden work and FEEL, one part riding lesson, one part experiential learning session, and two parts ceremony. There will be a round pen made of river drift deep in the woods with gates that lead out into the forest in each of the four directions. Beyond that, water falls down a mountain and into the river below. Close enough to hear, close enough to carry our prayers out to sea.

Tonight it is raining. Tea and candlelight on the table as I write this. Outside the window, the horses stand with wet backs, waiting, their presence dreaming us alive.

We are pulling the future up out of the ground. Somewhere from where there is the sound of dancing. Bone on horn and skin on hoof, the oldest words we know.

Smoke from a smudge hangs in the air. Lavender and wild Ontario sage. All of the tracks that have led us here.

She will carry me back across the threshold the same way she carried me in. Mree, the warrior mare who was mine all through adolescence, who continues to be mine in the edges between dreams. There is no tack on her save a red tasselled halter. My legs hang long off her back. Crow and eagle feathers are tied into her mane, blow in the wind as if they long to be free. We are standing at the edge where the West Coast of Canada begins to turn to liquid, falling into the wild heart of the Pacific Ocean.

The wind blows salt into our faces. A wet kiss that always makes me think of snow. We are at the confluence: where the river meets sound, sea, ocean, we stand as if a tree. Rooted. Our breath gathers around our heads like a cloud. We are praying with every inhalation; with every exhalation learning how much we can love. How much we can forgive. How much we can love.

Far, far off, a wet slap sounds against the surface of the water. The slow exhalations of a great and ancient creature dreaming through the waves just off the coast. A humpback whale. Mist rises from the water and wraps up against the edges of the mountains and covers us in its blanket. Sight disappears. Leaving the world soft, grey, nascent, waiting to be born again. From this moment onwards, we must know the way blind. Must trust in the threads of synchronicity, grief, love: trust that others are moving with us, just beyond the edges of the veil.

The white mare paws, testing for the edge with her hoof, for where night air meets dark water, where fresh water meets salt. Where all this rain fallen off the shoulders of mountains meets the edge of the world.

I am motionless on her back, waiting. I trust her. She has carried me, will carry me. Farther than the ground that meets my life.

The mare paws again. And then enters the cold waters of the Sound, her hooves stirring luminary trails through the phosphorescence that lights our way like the tail of a slow burning comet, her tail washed out behind her, swimming for distant islands.

Photo Credit Pat Robinson

Kera Willis

A writer, nomad, and lifelong horsewoman, Kera Willis received her Facilitator of Equine Experiential Learning Certificate from Horse Spirit connections in 2010, and in 2013 completed an intensive apprenticeship to become a certified practitioner of Horse Boy Method, a form of therapeutic riding specific to autism and other neurological conditions. She founded Mountain Horse School in 2012, where she combines a wide variety of traditional and cutting-edge equine modalities with the creative arts, shamanism, and earth-centric wisdom to create truly unique, heart-centered, and transformative experiences. She is currently working as Special Needs Assistant at the Whistler Waldorf School, and will begin offering sessions in Squamish Valley, BC in the spring of 2015.

For more information, please visit www.mountainhorseschool.com, or her blog: www.centreofthemovingworld.wordpress.com

CHAPTER 11

Where the Magic Begins

By Wendy Golding

FEEL is a new way of being in relationship for horses and people. It is a place of discovery and reflection which touches the deepest part of our human spirit. It is that part of our self that restores our wonder at the world and awakens our belief in magic, dreams, and possibilities.

The FEEL (Facilitated Equine Experiential Learning)® Alumni Association is proud to sponsor this book and present these inspirational stories highlighting the extraordinary connection between two species—horses and humans.

The FEEL Alumni is comprised of passionate women and men who are graduates of the intensive FEEL Certification Program. Their love and fascination of horses drew them to learn about a deeper connection with these magical beings. These courageous people were challenged to change the way they had been taught to think about horses; challenged to re-look at the traditional role of humans in our relationship with horses.

Becky and Ginger

A recent graduate, Becky, shared (with a huge grin on her face) an amazing story of how her relationship with her horse, Ginger, had changed after she took the teachings of the FEEL program back to her horses. After five years, Becky THOUGHT there was a strong relationship between the two of them; that she knew Ginger's personality, what she liked and what she didn't like. She thought they had a good partnership because Ginger did what she wanted when asked. Applying the new teachings, Ginger gradually assumed a brand-new personality–one Becky had never seen before. Ginger became who she truly was without the need to be who and what her owner expected her to be. There was a new light in her eye, an alertness; she was more tuned in to Becky and her surroundings, at times she chose to do things on her own, she explored her world with more interest and curiosity. She became more expressive in her language and her communication; she shook her head up and down if she agreed with something Becky said or licked and chewed if she wanted Becky to pay attention to something that was occurring in the moment. Ginger expressed her displeasure very clearly with pinned ears, a shake of the head, or a quick flick of the tail. From this place of authenticity both the human and the horse were able to create and collaborate together. They danced with life!

As one of the FEEL Alumni Steering Committee members, I am so grateful and honored to give voice to the unfolding story of the horse as teacher and healer. Our original vision of FEEL has grown extensively and impacted the lives of so many people and horses. It is wonderful to be a part of a community of like-minded people who come together with such a strong passion to make the world a better place. This is a family who is authentic with themselves and each other.

What is FEEL (Facilitated Equine Experiential Learning)?

FEEL is a leading-edge modality for learning more about yourself through personal discovery where the horse is honoured as our partner and teacher. In safe and gentle interactions with horses, people gain self-knowledge and acquire skills leading to positive life changes.

FEEL began in 2005 at Horse Spirit Connections, a not-for-profit corporation, with Wendy Golding and Andre Leclipteux. Even after thousands of horse sessions, the magic remains. Each time a person and a horse come together, the experience is new, profound, and life-changing. Wendy and Andre founded the FEEL Certification Training Program in 2008 to explore, expand, and share the incredible teachings of the horses and from there the FEEL Alumni was born.

FEEL Alumni

The FEEL Alumni is a membership-based, not-for-profit association of FEEL graduates who come together to foster the partnership and spiritual connection with horses.

The FEEL Alumni VISION is: To create and hold a sacred space of possibility where horses and FEEL graduates build a dynamic, authentic community to co-create and empower one another, strengthen the horse-human bond and give a voice to the wisdom and spirit of the horse.

The FEEL Approach

- We foster a collaborative, respectful relationship with horses

- We believe it is essential to connect through our hearts rather than our minds

- We consider horses to be a teacher or co-therapist (rather than a therapeutic tool or means to an end)

- We appreciate each horse as unique and individual

- We understand horses mirror our truth and authentic expression

- We recognize the synergistic connection between horses and humans allows for the collective raising of consciousness

The horses engage us in Experiential Learning–learning by doing. It is a process through which individuals gain knowledge, acquire skills, and enhance values from direct "felt" experiences in specially designed activities engaging with the horse on the ground.

FEEL Practitioners work with the primary healing energy of the relationship between horse and human. The Practitioners' role is to bridge communication between our two species and restore confidence to the person of their ability to sense, feel, and know their own truth. The horses are the natural teachers in the space, and more often than not, the power of what happens is in the purity of direct heart communication between horse and human. Depending on the FEEL Practitioners' education and scope of practice, Practitioners will practice Equine Facilitated Learning (EFL) or Equine Facilitated Psychotherapy (EFP).

Equine Facilitated Psychotherapy (EFP) is a powerful and effective therapeutic approach maximizing the partnerships of the therapist/ facilitator with the horse as teacher. This dynamic therapy helps people confront their fears and heal their wounds, reconnecting them with their natural ability to heal.

Equine Facilitated Learning (EFL) is based on an emotionally intimate partnership with the horse where the greatest potential for health and well-being can be found. Experiential horse activities, incorporating mindfulness techniques, foster those light-bulb moments of personal discovery leading to positive life changes.

As FEEL Practitioners we have noticed time and time again, that the horses can open up levels of healing the people have never experienced before. Heartfelt testimonials and grateful feedback continue to affirm the healing and the transformation that happens when horses and people come together with a felt experience.

How can Horses help you?

The horses help you become the kind of person you have always wanted to be. They teach you how to create harmony and balance in your life by aligning your mind, body, and spirit. Living from a place of heart brings such joy and freedom. Learning to connect with the spirit of the horse invites you to become one with your own spirit where you feel a sense of connectivity and closeness with all that is.

The horses support the discovery of who you really are–what we call your authentic self, by breaking down the layers of what society has said you have to be or what key influencers in your life have told you who you are. You don't need to wear a mask with the horses–they see and respond to the genuine person inside. So many times, when someone asks us how we are, we smile and politely say "fine." However inside, we may be feeling anger or another emotion coursing through our body. With the horse's incredible sensitivity to energy, the horse will respond to that strong emotion inside you, instead of the composed face you are showing to the world. Not only will the horse sense that emotion, the horse will give you the space to understand the message behind that emotion and release it at a deep cellular level.

Amy and Monty

Amy was someone who had suffered deep seated trauma from the time she was a young girl. Many mental health concerns surfaced as she struggled to survive in the world she was born into. In adulthood, she went to many therapists to understand and manage her pain. It wasn't until she found a horse therapist that deep healing started to happen. One of her horse therapists was named Monty who was a very wise and venerable teacher. Horses don't usually use their voice in a therapy session and when they do it is a nicker or a neigh not a high-pitched scream. However on this occasion, Monty was using his voice to encourage Amy to use hers. He sensed the anger and absolute rage that had been stuffed deep inside her body through years of abuse. Monty started to scream, it was so loud and stringent, the sound reverberated deep in their bodies. His cry mirrored how he wanted her to release the pent up anger through her voice; knowing her voice needed to be powerful and strong. Needless to say, hearing Monty doing an intense scream was shocking to Amy and the facilitator. Grounding quickly, the facilitator understood that Monty was being a teacher, as this was very unusual behavior on his part. Communicating this to Amy, the suggestion was to imitate Monty and join him. Monty screamed again, placed himself between Amy and the other participants, and encouraged her to release this harmful feeling. Taking her strength initially from Monty, Amy allowed her throat to open and her own screams came forth. Monty joined her until she was complete. In the utter silence that followed, Amy stood still beside Monty and allowed herself to feel her body, to go into her heart, and feel what it was like to be without pain. Amy discovered that working with horses, who had no judgment and no agenda, felt utterly safe for her. She shared that more healing took place in one session with a horse than months of traditional therapy. Amy accelerated her healing path with the help of the horses and found joy!

You can better understand your own behaviour when it is reflected by the horse as they are perfect mirrors for you to see how you create your current reality. Interestingly, this work with the horses attracts many people who are fascinated by horses but have a deep fear of them. It is amazing to watch someone so afraid of horses, who after just one session, is able to stand a foot away from the horse and do a profound heart connection with this huge being so much bigger than they are. From approaching the horse with trepidation and shaky footsteps, to feeling an incredible sense of peace and calm, they stroke the horse's body with rhythmic movements. Taking this same courage back into their lives enables them to face other fears from this place of newfound confidence in themselves.

As a sophisticated herd animal, horses immediately begin building relationships with people as they would a member of their own herd. Engaging with horses allows you to create a relationship with a being who offers unconditional support and love without judgment, where intimate, profound moments foster transformation and healing at a deep level.

Tom and Paris

Paris is a horse who provided loving support for a man named Tom, allowing him to heal his heart from the pain of lifelong prejudice and childhood sorrow. Tom came for an intensive two-day session with his family, his hope for healing was for his teenage stepdaughter. The true healing happened for him which opened up the space for a better relationship with his wife and children. The intensive was arranged by his wife and he was admittedly quite skeptical about what would happen with the horses. He met Paris in the barn and magic started to unfold. There was something in Tom's heart that was ready to heal and Paris was there to support him in all ways. It was like Paris held him in her arms, there was so much nurturing, loving energy for him. Later in a reflective session, Paris held the space for Tom to speak out loud his innermost, deep feelings. He was able to release the pain, the shame, and guilt he had carried for many years, with a being who could feel his soul and provide unconditional love. Paris was so attentive and protective of Tom; she stepped closer to Tom and moved around him so he couldn't be seen by anyone. This protective shield allowed Tom's healing tears to flow faster. Paris stood very still and her breathing became deeper and deeper until Tom came to a place of peaceful acceptance. With reluctance, Tom left Paris but he was transformed –he was lighter and more hopeful–he could provide the support for his stepdaughter to find her way in the world.

Creating a relationship with a horse involves much more than our simple desire to have one. Horses demand respect and authenticity each time we engage with them. They expect us to be fully present with them every moment. Animal Assisted Therapy is a broad umbrella that incorporates working with a variety of animals: dogs, cats, horses, rabbits to name a few. Because of the horses' sensitive prey nature, they are very different in their response to us than dogs are. When you come home, your dog will wag its tail and lick your face, uplifting you with their pure joy of seeing you home again. Horses on the other hand, pick up on your energy and your mood, and will respond to you accordingly. This is incredibly challenging but also a place of huge learning–so often we are not in the "here and now" but thinking about the future or the past causing us to miss magical, intimate moments with those around us and ourselves. With the horse in a teaching role, a simple leading exercise becomes a rich metaphor for how we lead our life.

Helen and Thor

Helen, a middle-aged woman, who was not sure of her role anymore, was asked to lead Thor to a pylon in the arena. Thor is a big, black Percheron nicknamed Gentle Giant. Given simple directions on how to lead a horse safely, Helen hesitantly took the lead rope and looking back at Thor, started to walk towards the pylon. Thor, sensing Helen's uncertainty, planted his feet and refused to move. He chose to be a teacher in this moment and when Thor decides not to move, no human can force him to do so. Helen continued to encourage and ask Thor to move, however her body language clearly stated that she did not expect him to follow her. Her shoulders were slumped forwards, her voice weak, her body continually looking back to see if Thor was following her. Tears of frustration started to well up. With some simple words of encouragement, Helen reconnected with Thor and restated out loud her intent. Still he would not budge. With more encouragement, she voiced her intent in a voice of power, pulling from a place deep within herself. This time Helen found that place of determination inside her belly and walked forwards with confidence, eyes on her goal. Now Thor willingly walked with her towards the pylon and had a beautiful connection with her as she completed the exercise. He put his massive head very gently on her belly and then her heart to emphasize this is the place where Helen will find that strength and determination. Helen went home with a strong resolve to be her own leader; this is the role she wanted to live. Horses can be our best therapists and encourage us to stand in our power and shining!

Horses help us embrace an inner wisdom more commonly known as our intuition. As children, we naturally listen to our bodies and delight in the ease through which we flow through our days. As we get older, the focus for learning and knowledge is from our minds. In today's fast-paced society, our emphasis is wholly concentrated on our mind to try and keep up. The more we focus on the brain in our head, the more we are out of balance and lose harmony. Horses have been gifted with a keen perception and just being in their presence reactivates our own body knowing. Trusting your intuition brings back a sense of belief and knowing allowing valuable insights to help you navigate your world.

Equine assisted healing is rapidly gaining credibility as people whisper about their magical experiences with these majestic creatures. While scientists and doctors are continually finding new evidence to describe and confirm how this relationship with the horses manifests change–***the horses continue to demonstrate it works over and over again!***

Jackie Leforet with the stallion energy of Franco.
In stillness she hears his voice singing into her heart

*Melissa Gordon inviting Bella to share with
her a beautiful and serene moment*

You can feel Lydia's joy as she embraces her incredible teacher

*Wendy teaching Thor how to sound the heartbeat
of Mother Earth through the drum*

Cheryl Emery feels the compassionate and strong energy of this gentle giant

What is it about the horse?

Horses are prey animals and this affects how they are built, how they learn, how they respond to their environment, how they protect and defend themselves, and how they socialize. What does it mean to be a prey animal? A prey animal is hunted by predators which means they are always ready to be in a state of flight. To ensure their species survival through millions of years, horses have been gifted with highly sensitive, observational skills and intuitive responses to their environment. Unlike humans who rely mainly on intellect, horses access the wisdom of their entire bodies, allowing them to read and respond to all the energies around them.

Horses are social animals with well-defined roles within their herds very similar to our family dynamics. They have distinct personalities with unique attitudes and approaches. They are exquisitely attuned to body language, innuendo, and emotional tone. An approach that works with one horse doesn't necessarily work with another, which invites us to expand our relational abilities as we partner with different horses.

The horses are experts in communication allowing people to learn how to communicate effectively with others within safe boundaries. Psychologist Albert Mehrabian[1] has determined that less than 7 percent of our communication is verbal. As such, horses help people understand their nonverbal cues, unconscious behaviour patterns, and the emotional import and intent of their words and actions. These qualities are so totally downplayed in our modern society that we are losing our ability to function fully and authentically in the moment. We are always communicating. Everything we think, feel, do, and say sends out a message. Horses help us become aware of how we communicate on every level—verbally, mentally, physically, and emotionally.

Horses are so sensitive and intelligent that we are only now acknowledging the wisdom they carry. Due to their highly advanced perception, they are very tuned into us and capable of acknowledging the slightest gestures we make and respond accordingly. In this way, as we make a change in our behavior or the way that we are feeling, we can see by the horse's behavior if the change was beneficial

The Cornerstones of FEEL

Relationship with Horses

Within FEEL we understand the horses to be teachers and honour the wisdom they bring to the human world. In this way we collaborate with the horses, understanding their role is absolutely KEY to the transformation and healing which happens. What does collaboration with the horse look like? It is an invitation between two beings who respect one another, connect through their whole body wisdom, and want to work together, bringing healing to humans and horses.

Each horse is an individual with its own personality, needs, and desires. We listen to the story of each horse, empathize with their feelings, and discover how they want to be involved with FEEL. Every horse, through its life experiences, has its own unique gift to bring to this work. One horse specializes in teaching young women how to set good boundaries for themselves; another is an expert at instilling confidence at a core level; another is dedicated to opening closed hearts; another delights in lifting spiritual awareness and encouraging someone to fly, and yet another is there to release that one tear that opens the floodgate for that person's healing tears. There is so much joy as we continue to create and evolve our relationship with these magical creatures.

Honouring the horse as teacher means that we understand that they have access to wisdom that is not available to humans. Working with horses allows humans to access this deeper connection, while not always understanding the specifics of what the horses are doing. Without that need to control and comprehend, we can open ourselves to the magic!

We strive to communicate with horses in their own language so they can be heard. They have an intricate non-verbal approach to imparting knowledge and provide an excellent role model for collaborative leadership. It is essential to be in a heart-centered relationship with these wise teachers. By providing them with "choice" in their day-to- day lives, horses redevelop their sentience. It is sad that so many domestic horses have learned to survive in the human world by doing what they are told to do. They no longer use the incredible knowledge they have access to. For generations mankind has treated horses as dumb animals; however nothing could be further from the truth. When a new horse arrives, the first thing that happens is to let the horse become a horse again. This can take anywhere from one month to two years depending on the trauma a horse has endured at the hands of humans.

Once a horse has awakened its sentience or natural wisdom, their natural therapeutic skills develop and expand. By attuning to a person's energy and paying attention to their emotional state and body language, horses actually listen to us at a much different and profound level. This resonance is a palpable sense of unity from one being to another. We encourage people to connect to horses through a heart connection as horses embody such huge hearts and bond through their powerful heart centers. Horses have a gentle way of bringing unconscious feelings to the surface creating the space for you to open your heart to both the dark and light parts of yourself. It is a time to feel your emotions and release them. Become whole again!

Horses of any age, size, or breed can make good FEEL partners. It is so heartwarming to see horses come back to life with a renewed sense of purpose after they were put out to pasture because they couldn't perform anymore. They have such big hearts and are so willing to be of service–another clear indication of that incredible bond that we share with them.

Relationship with Clients: As FEEL Practitioners we acknowledge that every person has the inherent right and ability to heal themselves. We encourage people to discover their own truths in a place of non-judgment–the teaching is so much more profound and lasting when people understand they are their own healers.

Creating a sacred place of possibility is crucial for both horses and people. A skilled facilitator forms a relationship based on trust where horses and humans have the willingness to feel vulnerable through being heard at a deep soul level.

Relationship with Themselves: Working with the horses in such deep connection, creates a demanding space where FEEL Practitioners are compelled to be heart centered and authentic with themselves and the horses. Horse teachers are honest and direct not only with the clients but with the facilitators themselves. In order to hold a space of sacred possibility for the best possible healing for the client, facilitators themselves have to be neutral and always willing to look at their own emotional fitness.

Emotions as a Language

Emotions are a vital connecting link between our body, mind, and spirit. They are fluid and carry large amounts of energy functioning as a tangible energetic force like a sound or smell that travels through the air. Our emotions are invisible, powerful, and full of information. You can walk into a room and feel a palpable sense of anger, fear, or grief without anyone having to say a word or acknowledging it.

Our culture has often denied or minimized the importance of emotions as a sense, and in fact has encouraged the suppression of so-called negative emotions. By reclaiming our emotions, we learn that emotions are neither positive nor negative, and that all emotions are equal in their ability to give us information about where we are in our lives, and what things need to be changed in order to bring us back into balance.

Horses are natural at having emotional agility. As prey animals, these sensitive, emotionally agile creatures have maintained over millions of years a highly developed ability to respond to subtle changes in stance, muscle tension, breathing, and feelings of other horses as well as people. Emotions can be transferred from one horse to many others instantaneously as energy, packed with information.

To the horses, emotions are simply information; they are not good or bad. They feel an emotion, it moves through them, and then they "go back to grazing." There isn't a lot of emotional residue, and unlike humans, horses do not repress emotions, or behave differently than they feel.

Horses transfer this emotional agility to people. When someone is "putting on a happy face" when actually they feel afraid, frustrated or angry, the horse can sense the true involuntary emotional energy through empathy and the person's body language. Horses will often mirror the precise emotion being suppressed and then calm down, the moment that the person simply acknowledges that feeling in themselves, even if the emotion is still there. When the mask is removed and authentic feelings are acknowledged, the horse is more relaxed. When a person becomes harmonious, the horse offers feedback. Horses are ideal coaches as they offer instant feedback to the changes we make to our behavior or the way we are feeling: This is one of the reasons FEEL is so effective.

Many of us are taught to fear our feelings; however, this only blocks our self-knowledge and inner truth. Our fears will recede if we allow our emotions to protect and inform us at a conscious level. We help people understand the language of emotions: the ability to use emotion as information, get the message behind the emotion, adjust our behaviour, relationship or environment, let the feeling go, and return to balance.

As we become more comfortable listening to our bodies, feeling our feelings, and asking ourselves what the message is behind our emotions, we become more emotionally intelligent and agile, more conscious. We become more like horses, able to read emotions as information and respond accordingly, not at the effect of our emotions and going into a reactive state.

Harmonizing Our Three Brains

We have three brains: our head, our heart, and our gut. Our heart and gut are often referred to as our second and third brains as they have more neural receptors than our mind making them far more powerful. As we become more conscious and acknowledge the messages from our heart and gut, it helps us make sense of our world.

When you stand beside a horse, look into his eye, connect with your heart, and stroke his velvety muzzle, your heart opens; a feeling of pure love pools in your chest, and the tactile sense from your fingers allows you to feel sensations of softness. From here the feelings and sensations travel to your mind. In your mind the experience gets changed into words and then you can think about it in words. The mind only recycles the energy that comes from the feelings and sensations you experienced. The mind thinks, it does not know. You can only know through feeling or doing, not from thinking.

Our gut has learning and decision-making abilities–it is much more than just a digestive system. Have you ever had that feeling in your gut that something is just not right? Most of the time we disregard these feelings until we start to listen and trust the wisdom coming from our bodies. This is the place of your intuition which allows you to make decisions based on a knowing not logic.

The heart is also much more than just an organ pumping blood throughout our bodies. The heart has neurons allowing memories to be stored in our heart center and it provides a continuous two-way dialogue between the brain and the rest of the body. When you have a direct experience, it does not go directly to the brain in your head. The first place it goes is to the neurological network of your gut and heart. Having these "felt" experiences allows you to start trusting the information from your heart and natural instincts.

Horses have both larger, more sensitive guts and expanded heart fields, thus creating much larger areas for receiving and responding to information. However, their neo-cortex, the part of the brain responsible for learning and higher thought, is not as developed as humans. Thus, horses are more likely to embody empathy and intuition rather than logic from their mind brain.

Just being around horses initiates a sense of deeper awareness, enhanced perspectives, and richer creativity. These huge beings invite mindfulness–paying attention in the present moment. This is an incredible gift, as humans tend to agonize over the past and worry about the future, missing so much of the richness of what is happening right now.

More than anything else, the horses teach us to be in the moment and to access our heart center and gut. In an article published by Kathleen Barry Ingram[2], the work with the horses allows a client to thrive instead of just survive. While the neocortical brain can rapidly process information, without the whole body (being the brain in the heart and the gut), only the minds' thoughts and information change.

The horses help you fully engage with the whole of who you are, creating lasting results through new neural pathways.

The horses create the space and experience for us as humans to increase our consciousness by harmonizing our three brains so they work together as a cohesive team leading to a harmonious and balanced life.

Deep Heart Connections

Horses teach us to "listen" from our heart where we hear and resonate with the truth of something. Just being in the presence of a horse creates magic; people have expressed so many different emotions, some they have never spoken of to another living soul; healing tears start to flow down the cheeks not only of women but men; people get in touch with their dreams again; they feel a bond with these incredible creatures that has no description.

On more practical terms the heart is much more than a muscular pump; it is a highly evolved organ of perception and communication. Heart neurons are directly connected to the brain producing a direct exchange of information. The heart also has its own memory which affects our consciousness and behavior, how we perceive the world.

The Heart Math Institute[3] has conducted ongoing research into the energy emanating and being received by the human heart which affects our moods, attitudes, and feelings–whether we are conscious of it or not. The heart is the most powerful generator of electromagnetic energy in the human body. The heart's electromagnetic field becomes more coherent as consciousness shifts from the brain to the heart. The more coherent the field, the more potent the information exchange. A coherent heart affects the brain wave pattern not only of the person achieving coherence, but also of any person with whom it comes into contact. The two fields begin to entrain or resonate with each other, opening a gateway of healing and empathy.

The Heart Math Institute has also performed research with humans and horses. They found that the electromagnetic field of the horse is five times stronger than that of a human's and the heart rate of a horse is three times slower. The horse naturally lives in a state of heart coherence and just being near a horse, we as humans can resonate with this deep energy. If we attain that place of heart resonance with a horse our bodies go into an alpha state similar to meditation.

In FEEL activities, people are encouraged to experience this incredible heart connection between a horse and themselves. For some, it is experienced as 'feeling felt,' pure love, compassion, peace, connection to something more, the mystery of life, or a sharing of soul essence. To see a young man, 12 years old, experience his first heart connection with a horse was exquisite! This was his first time with a horse, yet he was able to stand next to this horse in a place of trust and shut his eyes in front of his peers. There was such a palpable connection between both of them that it brought tears to the eyes of everyone watching. After thanking the horse, he walked towards me with the biggest grin on his face and gave me a giant hug, saying it was the best experience of his life!

Spiritual Consciousness

Looking deep into a horse's eye lets you touch your soul.

Horses teach you

the rhythm of the dance of life.

They surround you with Joy

As you listen to the murmur

Of the voice of Spirit in your heart.

—Author unknown

Spirituality encapsulates an understanding of the world as greater than what can be seen, felt, heard, or understood. Horses invite us into another world—they show us our higher self and give us ways to access our greatest potential providing a powerful pathway to reconnect with divine consciousness.

Our connection with horses stimulates a deeply buried aspect of nature within us and rekindles a lost connection to that something greater–our collective wisdom.

This is an evolution of higher consciousness for humans precipitated by the sentient awareness of horses. Horses have an intelligence and awareness that is beyond our current ability to comprehend. Horses physically, emotionally, and spiritually have a higher vibrational frequency than humans. When we are in this place of higher vibration with the horse, our human hearts and bodies can entrain this higher frequency on all levels. Together horse and human travel to higher levels of consciousness.

Horses have existed on planet earth for millions of years retaining an uncanny connection with their ancestors and maintaining the instincts and behaviour of their ancient lineage. This archetypical model supports the idea of a collective memory. Each individual horse both draws upon and contributes to this collective memory of the species. This means that new patterns of behaviour can spread more rapidly than would otherwise be possible–horses from one herd can be connected to another herd thousands of miles away. Horses around the world are hearing the call to become healers!

This connection to a species consciousness also leads to a sharing of divine awareness between horse and human. Not only does this lead to humans realizing a higher spiritual potential, it fosters for the horses a higher level of awareness of their own species' wisdom. This harmonizing of wisdom continues to expand the bonds between horses and humans and journeying together to a realm of new possibilities.

Being in relationship with horses you will experience:

Expanded awareness
Opening of your heart
Strengthening your intuition
Understanding subtle boundaries
An increase of vitality and energy

Discover the magic of who you are and heal your heart through the wisdom of the Horse.

The Horses are Calling You!

For People Who Dream With Horses

If you feel inspired from these stories, we invite you to meditate and call in horse energy to experience the magic for yourself. Make yourself comfortable in a quiet space or in nature. Breathing deeply, allow your body and most importantly your mind to become tranquil and still. Focus your attention on your heart center, allowing your heart to open. Ask for a spirit horse to come. You may see, hear, or just feel the presence of this mystical creature. Ask your sage horse for words of wisdom to help you in your life's journey, then with permission, jump on your horses back, and go for a ride. Feel the power of the horse's body between your legs, and allow yourself to be transported to another world. Let your horse lead the way with his innate wisdom and let his movement free your soul! Coming back to earth, ask for any final insights, before you thank your horse.

For People with Horses

We have included a special invitation from the horses to deepen the bond you have with your horses. With your horse, go for a walk together. Allow enough time so there is no pressure. Holding your horse with a loose lead rope, start doing conscious breathing. Take nice, big breaths, breathing in from your nose and exhaling through your mouth. After the first deep breath, visualize or imagine you are exhaling your breath, your life force, through your heart, your belly, and your feet in turn. You will feel your breath traveling through and grounding your body. From this place, take a casual stroll and talk out loud with your best friend, your horse. Listen and see how your horse engages you in conversation. Learn to engage with the "language of horse" through your heart. At the end of your walk, take off the halter so your horse is at liberty in a safe place and spend time with your horse in intimate connection asking and expecting nothing from each other. Allow yourself to just BE and let the magic continue!

247

Calling All Healers

In this time of shifting consciousness and awakening, the horses may be calling you to explore this powerful and transformational healing modality. Find a FEEL Practitioner near you to partner with, so you too can bring the magic of the horses together with your unique healing gifts and see the incredible results with your clients. OR is it time for you to explore becoming a FEEL Practitioner yourself?

We invite you to contact the amazing authors in this book and visit their gifted horses to experience the magic firsthand! They have spent countless hours compiling their compelling stories in order to share their heartfelt experiences with you. Locate them through their contact information found at the end of each chapter.

www.FEELAlumni.com will take you to our FEEL Alumni Graduates.

Find a FEEL Practitioner near you and experience for yourself the life changing power of horses.

CHAPTER NOTES

Chapter 3

1 *Horse as Teacher*, Wendy Golding, Teaching the Wisdom of the Horse Ancestors,125,126

Chapter 6

1 Carlos Castenada, *The Power of Silence*, Washington Square Press, 1987, page 149

2 National Geographic, February 2009

3 Linda Kohanov, *Way of the Horse*, New World Library, 2007 pages 147 – 148

Chapter 8

Online; The Psychology Dictionary by Kendra Cherry Psychology Expert

Eckman, P. (1999), Basic Emotions, in Dalgleish, T; Power, M, Handbook of Cognition and Emotion. Sussex, UK: John Wiley & Sons

Hockenburry, D.H. & Hochenburry, SE. (2007) Discovering Psychology. New York; Worth Publishers

Plutchik, R. (1980). Emotion, theory, research, and experience: vol. 1. Theories of emotion 1. New York: Academic

Chapter 9

1 Linda Kohanov, Way of the Horse, (Novato, Calif.: New World Library, 2007), p. 197

2 Caroline Myss, Daily Message Archives, http://www.myss.com/library/dailymess

Chapter 10

1 Lewis Carol. *The Horse and His Boy.* (Lions, 1989).

2 Horse Boy Method. Web page. (www.horseboyworld.com).

3 Neurodivergent K. "What Autism Really Is," http://thisisautismflashblog.blogspot.ca/, Nov. 18 2014

4 Linda Kohanov. *The Tao of Equus: A Woman's Journey of Healing and Transformation Through the Way of the Horse.* (Novato, Cali.: New World Library, 2001).

5 Naoki Higashida and David Mitchell. The Reason Why I Jump. (Random House, 2013).

6 Heal With Horses Therapeutic Centre. Web page. (www.healwithhorses.ca).

7 Henry Beston. *The Outermost House: A Year of Life on the Great Beach of Cape Cod.* (New York, NY: Henry Holt and Company, 2003).

Chapter 11

1 Psychologist Albert Mehrabian, Institute of Judicial Studies Handout 1, Albert   Mehrabian Communication Studies, 1.

2 Kathleen Barry Ingram, the work with the horses..., Article Implicit Knowing versus Explicit Knowledge And Equine Facilitated Learning, 5.

3 The Heart Math Institute, www.heartmath.org

CPSIA information can be obtained at www.ICGtesting.com
Printed in the USA
LVOW04s0458160415

434745LV00013B/115/P